PHRASEBOOK

Hadrien Dhont
Carrie Stipic Fawcett
Dr William Liller
Naomi C. Losch
Teata Makirere
Fepulea'i Lasei Vita John Mayer
Ana Betty Rapahango
Michael Simpson
Darrell Tryon

South Pacific phrasebook
  1st edition – September 1999

Published by
Lonely Planet Publications Pty Ltd A.C.N. 005 607 983
192 Burwood Rd, Hawthorn, Victoria 3122, Australia

Lonely Planet Offices
Australia PO Box 617, Hawthorn, Victoria 3122
USA 150 Linden St, Oakland CA 94607
UK 10a Spring Place, London NW5 3BH
France 1 rue du Dahomey, 75011 Paris

Front cover illustration
  Lobster Claw Heliconia Etcetera by Brendan Dempsey

ISBN 0 86442 595 3

text and maps © Lonely Planet Publications 1999
cover illustration © Lonely Planet 1999

Printed by The Bookmaker Pty Ltd
Printed in China

About the Authors

Hadrien Dhont

Hadrien Dhont is a student of Kanak Languages at INALCO, Paris.

Carrie Stipic Fawcett

Carrie Stipic Fawcett is a former US Peace Corps volunteer for Niue. After gaining a bachelor of Science from the College of William and Mary in Virginia, she lived and worked in Niue for three years assisting in the development of information systems.

Naomi C. Losch

Naomi C. Losch has been teaching at the University of Hawaii at Manoa since 1994. Before that, she worked on the Ethnological Collection at the Bishop Museum. She has been teaching Hawaiian language and culture at tertiary level since 1968, and taught at Leeward Community College for 24 years.

Te 'Atamira

Te 'Atamira, also known as Ta Makirere, spent his early childhood on Aitutaki before moving to Rarotonga, then on to New Zealand to train as a teacher. He returned to Rarotonga, and after a year with the Legislative Assembly as the official interpreter and translator of government business, he and his wife moved to Aitutaki to teach at the junior high school. Four years later, he went to theological college in Fiji and, after a few years in the ministry, helped launch a communications program for the Pacific Conferences on Churches in Suva. Back in Rarotonga, he worked as Editor of the Cook Islands' daily newspaper, then for the Education Department, and later as Editor of Parliamentary Debates for the government of the Cook Islands. Now retired, he teaches ukulele, guitar and Maori.

Fepulea'i Lasei Vita John Mayer

John Mayer worked in Western Samoa from 1970 to 1976 as a Peace Corps Volunteer and Samoan language specialist. Since 1976, he has coordinated the Samoan Language and Culture Program at the University of Hawaii at Manoa. He has led seven University Study Abroad Programs to the island of Manono, and holds the matai titles of Fepulea'i from the island of Savai'i and Lasei from the island of Manono.

Ana Betty Rapahango

Ana Betty Rapahango is a native-born Rapanui who lives in mainland Chile. She is the director of the William Mulloy Library, currently located at the Fonck Society Museum in Vina del Mar, Chile.

Dr William Liller

Dr William Liller is a professional astronomer, formerly of Harvard University. Now a resident of Chile, he is on the Board of Directors of the Easter Island Foundation. He has published several books about Easter Island.

Michael Simpson

Michael Simpson moved from New Zealand to Tonga with his family at the age of six. He's currently studying for a degree in Pacific Languages at the University of the South Pacific, while working at Lavengamalie College in Tonga.

Darrell Tryon

Darrell Tryon is a linguist at the Research School of Pacific and Asian Studies at the Australian National University, Canberra. He is the author of a number of publications on Polynesian languages, including *Conversational Tahitian*.

From the Authors

Carrie Stipic Fawcett would like to thank Sifa Ioane for her dedication to preserving the Niuean langauge and for assisting the US Peace Corps volunteers in their language pursuits. She'd also like to thank her host family, Billy and Losa Talagi and their children for making her part of their family.

Naomi C. Losch would like to thank John Mayer, a good friend and colleague, for his kind support and encouragement.

Ta Makirere expresses his sincere gratitude to his 'adopted' daughter Leata Kollart, for typing and for her devotion, and especially for her patience in correcting the computer settings each time he made a mess of them. He'd also like to thank Jane Lamb for making her computer accessible to Leata and for sending messages, and Ardavan and Fariba Motlagh for their help with their computer. To anybody who had a bit in this work, he says Meitaki Maata.

John Mayer would like to give special acknowledgements to High Chief Fepulea'i Vita Tanielu, Samoan language lecturer at the University of Hawaii at Manoa, for reviewing his chapter and for his valuable cultural insights.

Ana Betty Haoa Rapahango and Dr William Liller are grateful to the many people who've helped with this project, and give their thanks especially to Rafael Haoa, Dr Steven R. Fischer and Dr Georgia Lee.

Michael Simpson would like to thank his mother for her support and encouragement, and the staff of LP for their patience and helpfulness.

Darrell Tryon wishes to express his thanks and appreciation to his many Polynesian friends throughout French Polynesia for generously sharing their language and culture with him.

From the Publisher

Norfolk English words and phrases were taken from Beryl Nobbs Palmer's *A Dictionary of Norfolk Words and Usages*, with the kind permission of John Palmer. Ray and Eileen Young supplied the Pitkern words and phrases, and placenames were provided by Paul Lareau. Thanks to Paul Geraghty for proofreading the Fijian chapter, Wharepapa Savage for proofreading and giving advice on the Maori chapter, and Dick Nowell for translating the Kanak chapter. Thanks to Darrell Tryon, Ana Betty Rapahango, Dr William Liller and Hadrien Dhont for providing information for the introduction. The sections on Fijian Hindi, Pacific French, Spanish and New Zealand English were compiled at Lonely Planet.

Brendan Dempsey drew the luscious cover illustration, Jules Chapple illustrated the book and Jim Miller lent his mapping expertise. Joanne Adams ably handled layout and design, Vicki Webb edited and compiled the introduction, Renée Otmar proofread and Sally Steward and Peter D'Onghia held it all together.

CONTENTS

INTRODUCTION 11

Abbreviations 14   Map 12

FIJIAN 15

Map 16   Getting Around 35
Introduction 17   Festivals 39
Pronunciation 19   Time & Dates 41
Meeting People 22   Numbers 42
Food 32   Health 44

HAWAIIAN 47

Map 48   Holidays & Festivals 63
Introduction 49   The Hula 65
Pronunciation 50   Myths & Legends 68
Meeting People 51   Time & Dates 69
Food 55   Numbers 70
Getting Around 57

KANAK LANGUAGES 71

Map 72   Festivals 81
Introduction 73   Time & Dates 83
Pronunciation 75   Numbers 86
Meeting people 76   The Ajie language 87
Food 79   The Nengone language 90
Getting Around 80

MAORI 93

Map 94   Getting Around 104
Introduction 95   Legends 108
Pronunciation 96   Time & Dates 112
Meeting People 98   Numbers 114
Food 104

NIUEAN 117

Map	118	Getting Around	129
Introduction	119	Celebrations	131
Pronunciation	120	Time & Dates	133
Meeting People	123	Numbers	135
Food	128		

RAPANUI 137

Map	138	Getting Around	145
Introduction	139	Festivals	152
Pronunciation	140	Legends	155
Meeting people	142	Time & Dates	157
Food	144	Numbers	158

RAROTONGAN MAORI 161

Map	162	Getting Around	168
Introduction	163	Festivals	171
Pronunciation	163	Legends	173
Meeting People	164	Time & Dates	174
Food	166	Numbers	175

SAMOAN 177

Map	178	Food	193
Introduction	179	Getting Around	195
Pronunciation	180	Festivals & Holidays	201
Meeting People	183	Legends	203
Family & Social		Time & Dates	205
Structure	190	Numbers	206

TAHITIAN 209

Map	210	Getting Around	220
Introduction	211	Festivals	223
Pronunication	212	Music & Dance	224
English Influence	214	Legends	226
Modern Tahitian	214	Time & Dates	227
Meeting People	217	Numbers	228
Food	218		

TONGAN 231

Map 232
Introduction 233
Pronunciation 233
Meeting People 235
Food 242
Getting Around 244

Festivals 246
Dance 248
Myths & Legends 249
Time 251
Numbers 252

OTHER LANGUAGES 253

Map 254
Fijian Hindi 255
Pacific French 262

Spanish 270
Pacific Englishes 279

FURTHER READING 291

Fijian 293
Hawaiian 293
Maori 293
Rapanui 294
Rarotongan Maori 295

Samoan 296
Tahitian 298
Tongan 298
Other languages 299

INTRODUCTION

The languages in this book belong to the Austronesian language family (Austronesian meaning 'of the southern islands'), which includes languages spoken within a huge area from Madagascar in the west to Easter Island in the east, and from Hawaii in the north to New Zealand in the south. The Austronesian language family includes nearly all languages spoken on islands of the South Pacific, as well as the indigenous languages of Melanesia, Madagascar, Singapore, Malaysia, Taiwan, the Philippines, nearly all of Indonesia, and the coastal regions of Papua New Guinea.

Austronesian languages are believed to have originated on the southern China mainland, when the Han Chinese occupied only northern China. They are thought to have been spread when the original speakers migrated first to Taiwan, about 5000–6000 years ago, then on to the Philippines and Indonesia. From Indonesia, they were taken into Oceania, arriving in the New Britain–New Ireland region of Papua New Guinea about 4000 years ago.

From there they quickly spread through the Melanesian chain down to the Fiji Islands and out into Polynesia, reaching this area around 3000 years ago. After a period of stabilisation, they spread eastwards, reaching the Society Islands some 2000 years ago.

Austronesian languages can be divided into two branches. The Eastern branch, also known as 'Oceanic', is made up of languages from Polynesia, Melanesia (including Fiji and New Caledonia) and Micronesia. The Western branch includes languages from Indonesia, Malaysia, the Philippines and Madagascar.

Polynesian languages (Polynesia meaning 'many islands') are spoken over an area covering a total of around 8000km by 10,000km. Polynesia forms a triangle bounded by Hawaii, Easter Island and New Zealand, and also includes outlying islands scattered through Fiji and the East Indies. Polynesian languages include Hawaiian, Maori, Rarotongan Maori, Niuean, Rapanui, Samoan, Tahitian and Tongan. These languages are closely related, due to their relatively recent separation, and employ similar sounds and grammatical structures.

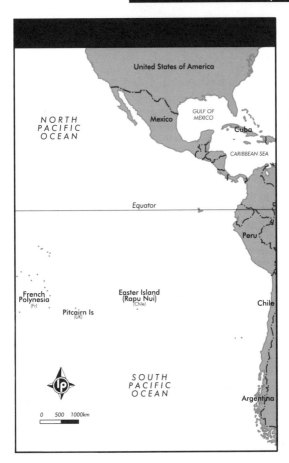

United States of America

NORTH
PACIFIC
OCEAN

Mexico

GULF OF
MEXICO

Cuba

CARIBBEAN SEA

Equator

Peru

French
Polynesia
(Fr)

Pitcairn Is
(UK)

Easter Island
(Rapu Nui)
(Chile)

Chile

SOUTH
PACIFIC
OCEAN

Argentina

0   500   1000km

	Rapanui	Tahitian	Samoan	Maori	Hawaiian
water	vai	vai	vai	wai	wai
love/ greeting	aroha	aroha	alofa	aroha	aloha
fish	ika	i'a	i'a	ika	i'a
large	nui	nui	nui	nui	nui
small	iti	iti	iti	iti	iti
chicken	moa	moa	moa	moa	moa

While it's usually possible to communicate in either English, French or Spanish on the islands of the South Pacific and Hawaii, knowing a little of the local language and terminology might help you learn more about and express an interest in the local people and their cultures.

ABBREVIATIONS USED IN THIS BOOK

dl	dual (refers to two people)
excl	exclusive (excludes the person being addressed)
f	female
incl	inclusive (includes the person being addressed)
inf	informal
m	male
pl	plural
pol	polite

FIJIAN

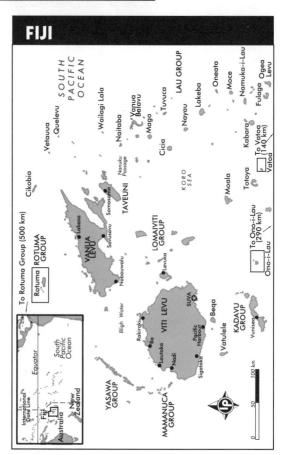

FIJIAN

INTRODUCTION

One of the reasons many visitors from the English-speaking world find Fiji such a congenial place to visit is because they don't have to learn another language – most local people who come into contact with tourists can speak English, and all signs and official forms are also in English.

At the same time, for almost all local people English is not their mother tongue – the majority of Fijians speak Fijian at home, while the second largest ethnic group, the Indians, speak Fijian Hindi (see page 255). If you really want to have a more-than-superficial knowledge of the Fijian people and their culture, it's important that you know something of the Fijian language. No matter how poor your attempts may be at first, you'll be greatly encouraged by the response from your Fijian friends. Fijians are remarkably tolerant of visitors' attempts to speak their language, and even if you've only managed to string a few words together, they'll tell you that you speak 'perfect' Fijian. Of course, if you want to leave the hotels and town centres to visit Fijians in their homes, whether in towns or villages, then some knowledge of Fijian is essential.

History

Fiji was probably originally settled some 3500 years ago, and the many regional dialects found in Fiji today all descend, at least partly, from the language spoken by the original inhabitants. They would have come from one of the island groups to the west, either the Solomons or Vanuatu, having left their South-East Asian homeland at least a thousand years previously, and spread eastwards by way of Indonesia, the Philippines and Papua New Guinea. From Fiji, groups left to settle the nearby islands of Rotuma, Tonga and Samoa, and from there they spread out to inhabit the rest of Polynesia, from Hawaii in the north to Rapa Nui (Easter Island) in the east, to Aotearoa (New Zealand) in the south. All of the people in this vast area of settlement speak related languages belonging to the language family known as 'Austronesian', the most widespread language family in the world.

Dialects

There are some 300 regional dialects of Fijian, all belonging to one of two major groupings. All varieties spoken to the west of a line extending north-south, with a couple of kinks, across the centre of Vitilevu (see page 16), belong to the Western Fijian group, while all others are Eastern Fijian.

Fortunately for the language learner, there is one variety which is understood by Fijians all over the islands, based on the Eastern varieties of the Bau-Rewa area, which was the major political centre in the 19th century, before Fiji became a British colony in 1874. This standard form of Fijian is popularly known as 'Bauan' (vosa vakabau), though linguists prefer to reserve this term for the language actually spoken on Bau, and refer to the standard variety as Standard Fijian. It is used in conversation among Fijians from different areas, on radio, TV and in schools, and is the variety used in this chapter. Note that this chapter focuses on spoken Fijian. The form traditionally used in writing, and in books and newspapers, is slightly different, but the differences are obvious and will present no difficulties. For instance, you'll often find ko written for o, and ki or e for i.

Standard Fijian isn't used exclusively by Fijians, but is also known to some extent by members of other communities in Fiji, especially in rural areas. Most Rotumans, Pacific Islanders and part-Europeans speak it fluently, and many Fijian Indians have a working knowledge of it, especially in places like the Sigatoka Valley, Levuka, Savusavu and Taveuni. So Fijian is a useful language to have anywhere in Fiji. Although not officially designated as such, it functions as a national language, and non-Fijians who do speak it are proud of the fact.

Foreigner Talk

There's a tradition in Fiji of using a simplified, baby-talk kind of language with non-Fijians, and you should be prepared for and recognise it. Its more conspicuous traits are the incessant use of the words sa and ko, which serve to mark speech as being 'foreigner talk', and the lack of prepositions. For example, the common question O lako i vei? 'Where are you going?' becomes

Ko iko sa lako vei?, and O kilai au? 'Do you know me?' becomes Ko iko sa kila ko yau? In many cases, you may just have to put up with it, but if the speaker is someone you talk with frequently, you might try asking them to vosa vakadodonu (speak properly).

> **BULA!**
>
> If someone sneezes, say bula! – if they sneeze again, tubu! 'grow!' or moli! 'health!'. They may thank you by saying moli once or a few times.

PRONUNCIATION

Fijian pronunciation isn't especially difficult for the English speaker, since most of the sounds are the same as English sounds. The standard Fijian alphabet uses all the English letters, except 'x'. The letters h and z occur only rarely, in borrowed words.

Since the Fijian alphabet was devised relatively recently (in the 1830s), and by a missionary who was also a very competent linguist, it's almost perfectly phonetic. That means that each letter has only one sound, and each sound is represented by only one letter. Once a small number of conventions are learned, Fijian is a dream to pronounce.

Vowels

As with all Pacific languages, the five Fijian vowels are pronounced much as they are in languages such as Spanish, German and Italian.

a	as the 'a' in 'father'
e	as the 'e' in 'bet'
i	as the 'ee' in 'machine'
o	as the 'o' in 'more'
u	as the 'oo' in 'zoo'

When two vowels appear together, they retain a pronunciation similar to their individual sounds.

FIJIAN

ai	pronounced like the 'y' in 'my'
ei	like the 'ay' in 'lay'
au	like 'ow' in 'now'

Vowels with macrons, such as ā, ē, ī, ō and ū, are pronounced significantly longer than the corresponding unmarked vowel. An approximate English equivalent would be the difference between the final vowel sound in 'icy' and 'I see'.

To get the right meaning of a word, it's important that the length be indicated. For example, mama means 'a ring', mamā means 'chew it', and māmā means 'light (in weight)'.

Fijians themselves rarely if ever write macrons, since they weren't part of the system of writing taught to them by the early missionaries, and in any case vowel length is often clear from the context. However, macrons are essential for the language learner, and for that reason are used throughout this chapter.

Vowels with an acute accent, such as ó, are are given stress.

Consonants

Most consonants are pronounced as they are in English, but a few differences need to be learned.

b	pronounced with a preceding nasal consonant, as *mb*
c	as the 'th' in 'this'
d	pronounced with a preceding nasal consonant, as *nd*
g	'ng' as in 'sing'
j	pronounced as the 'ch' in 'charm', but without a following puff of breath
k	as in English, but without a following puff of breath
p	as in English, but without a following puff of breath
q	'ng' as in 'angry'
r	trilled as in Scottish English or Spanish
t	without the following puff of breath; often pronounced 'ch' before 'i'
v	pronounced by placing the lower lip against the upper lip, not against the upper teeth as in English

FIJIAN

Occasionally on maps and in tourist publications, you'll find a variation on this spelling system which is intended to be easier for English speakers. In this system, Yanuca is spelt 'Yanutha', Beqa 'Mbengga' and so on.

Stress

It's quite easy to know which vowel to stress in Fijian. The rule is, if the final vowel is a long vowel, it is stressed. If not, the second last one is stressed. Because the rule is completely regular, there's normally no need to mark stress in Fijian.

Intonation

In most cases, the best way to learn intonation is simply to follow the intonation patterns of native speakers. Intonation is important in distinguishing between statements and yes/no questions since, unlike English, word order doesn't change for questions. Fortunately, the intonation for questions is similar to English, with the pitch of the voice rising towards the end of the sentence. Thus, kana with low pitch throughout is an order for someone to eat, whereas kana? with high rising pitch is a question meaning 'would you like to eat?'.

FIJIAN

HANDSHAKES

Shaking hands was introduced to Fiji in the 19th century by way of Tonga, and quickly became the established custom (the word for shaking hands, lūlulu, is borrowed from the Tongan 'lulululu'). An affectionate handshake can be very long, and may even last throughout an entire conversation. When introduced to a high chief, it's the Fijian custom to sit or crouch down immediately after the handshake, bow the head, and cobo (clap with hollowed hands) three or more times. This isn't required of non-Fijians.

MEETING PEOPLE
Greetings

The all-purpose greeting in Fiji is bula (lit: live), which corresponds to 'hello', 'pleased to meet you' and 'how are you?'.

Hello. (to two people)	Drau bula.
Hello. (to a group of people)	Dou bula.
Hello. (to a large number of people, or to an adult who's a stranger or who has higher status)	Nī bula.

In reply, you may simply say either io or ia (a bit more respectful), or return the bula, or both (io, bula!).

If it's morning, use yadra (lit: wake) rather than bula as a greeting. As with bula, the reply is to simply say io or ia (a bit more respectful), or return the yadra, or both (io, yadra).

When passing someone on the road or in a village, you should always greet them. A smile and a nod and an io will do, but a fuller greeting (bula or yadra) is nicer. After greeting, it's customary to inquire as to each other's movements.

The word moce (goodbye) is used to greet to strangers you pass in the evening or at night, or people passing in vehicles on their way to distant parts (at any time of the day) – O(nī) lai vei? 'Where are you going?'. Or, if you know that they're on their way home – O(nī) lesu mai vei? 'Where have you been?'.

Such questions may seem rude to English speakers, but in Fiji they're the custom. It's perfectly OK to give a very vague reply.

POLITE & INFORMAL

In Fijian, the suffix -nī is used to indicate polite speech. The polite form is used when speaking to adult strangers or to someone of higher social standing. The suffix -nī is shown in parentheses to give both informal and polite options.

RESPONDING TO INVITATIONS	
Thanks.	Vinaka. (accompanied by a nod)
Thank you very much.	Vinaka vakalevu; Vinaka sara vakalevu.
No thanks.	Vinaka. (accompanied by a shake of the head and/or an open palm)

I'm just going in this direction.   Au se lako/gole mada vāqō.

Nowhere in particular, just   Sega, lesu gā mai keā.
back from over there.

But if you wish to be more specific:

I'm going (to the) ...	Au se lako mada i ...
home	vale/neitou
hotel	na ōtela
shop	na sitoa

The se and mada are for politeness, and may be omitted, such as when you pass a friend. Gole is often used instead of lako.

When someone has told you where they're going or coming from, say vinaka 'thanks', and say where you're going to or coming from, if you haven't already done so, then say 'goodbye'.

If you're passing in a hurry or at a distance, smile and nod and point in the direction you're going.

Goodbyes

If you have to leave briefly but intend to return, say, Au na lesu tale mai 'I'll be back'.

To wrap up a conversation, say ia sā vinaka 'well thanks' or sa i koya 'that's it'. Next, state that you wish to leave, and perhaps add where you're going to: Au se lako/gole mada 'I'll be going now', or more politely, Au sā tatau meu sā lako or Au sā tatau meu sā lesu tale 'With your permission, I'll take my leave'.

FIJIAN

The reply is a word of thanks such as vinaka, io vinaka, sā vinaka or vinaka vakalevu.

If you're leaving someone's home, they'll probably invite you to stay for the next meal before you leave, by saying Tou katalau/ vakasigalevu/vakayakavi mada 'Please stay for breakfast/lunch/ dinner'. If you want to politely decline the invitation, again use a word of thanks such as vinaka.

The all-purpose word of farewell is moce (lit: sleep). As with bula and yadra, the reply is to simply say io or ia (a bit more respectful), or return the moce, or both (io, moce).

Announcing your departure and saying moce is only appropriate if you won't see that person again for a while. If you expect to meet the person again soon, you should say something like Au sā liu mada or Qai muri yani? 'See you later'. To which the reply is io 'yes', and possibly Au na qai muri yani 'I'll join you later'.

Finally, you may wish to send your regards or love with your departing guest. Loloma yani is the general expression – to specify, add vei, as in Loloma yani vei Jo 'Give my regards to Joe'.

FIJIAN

DID YOU KNOW ... Fiji has a small but strong community of poets, playwrights and other writers. Contemporary literature includes works by Joseph Veramu, the author of the short story collection *The Black Messiah* and the novel *Moving Through the Streets*, about urban teenagers in Suva. Jo Nacola's work includes the play *I Native No More*. The Fiji Writers Association has published *Trapped: A Collection of Writings from Fiji*.

FALSE FRIENDS

The vocabulary of Fiji English is derived mostly from New Zealand English, but there are some common words that have quite unexpected meanings.

Fiji English	English
bluff	lie; deceive; give a wrong answer
canvas	running shoes
grog	kava
step	cut school; wag; play truant
Good luck to ...!	It serves ... right!
Not even!	No way!

Forms of Address

Fijians usually have two names – a Christian name, taken from a saint or missionary, and a traditional Fijian name. One of these will be used as the common form of address. Some have also adopted the practice of having a family name, using the father's traditional name.

In some places, especially parts of the main island of Vitilevu, it's polite to call a married man tamai ... (father of ...) and a married woman tinai ... (mother of ...), adding the name of their eldest child.

People of standing in the community are often addressed by their office or their husband's office:

Good morning ...	(Nī) yadra ...
teacher	qasenivuli
minister (of religion)	na (tūraga) italatala
minister's wife	radinitalatala
doctor	vuniwai
doctor's wife	radinivuniwai

The word radini may also be used for the wife of any dignitary.

FIJIAN

Attracting Attention

To attract someone's attention from a distance, use a loud, sudden hiss. To beckon someone, wave with the palm downwards.

Excuse me!	Mai!
Come here! (to an adult stranger)	Kemunī!
I wonder if I might bother you?	Au kerekere mada.

To attract the attention of someone sitting next to you, it's customary to tap or scratch lightly a couple of times on their thigh. This can be a little alarming the first time it happens to you, so be prepared.

Apologies

A general word of apology, such as for keeping someone waiting, treading on their foot or knocking into them in the street, is (nī) vosota sara, or (nī) vosoti au. This may be preceded by an expression of annoyance with oneself and/or pity such as oilei or isa. If there's time to reply, say sega ni dua na kā 'it's nothing', or just sega. There's no need to apologise for belching.

REQUESTS

The usual way to broach a request is au kerekere mada. If it's a particularly difficult request, begin with (nī) yalovinaka 'be kind'. For instance, if you wish to ask a stranger not to smoke, it would be extremely rude to put the request directly, so say something like I kemunī, nī yalovinaka, e dau lako vakacā vei au na tavako 'excuse me, be kind, I'm allergic to tobacco'.

May I ...?	Au ... mada?
Excuse me. (may I go past you)	Au lako mada yani.
Sure. (you may go past me)	Mai.

A special word of apology, tilou or jilou, is used, often repeatedly, when you have to invade someone's space (as defined in Fijian culture), such as when pushing your way through a crowd, touching a part of someone's body (especially the head) or passing behind or in front of someone who is seated.

Sorry. (general)	(Nī) vosota sara;
	(Nī) vosoti au.
Sorry. (if invading space)	Tilou/Jilou.
It's nothing.	Sega ni dua na kā.

Body Language & Etiquette

A headshake means 'no', as in English. 'Yes' is more an upward nod of the head and/or raising the eyebrows.

As soon as you enter a house, sit down on the floor. When asked to move to another place in the house, crawl there, or walk stooping, remembering to say jilou as you pass people. If you need to stand up in a house to get something when people are sitting down, first ask permission (au se tarā mada na), then when you sit down again, cobo (clap with hollowed hands) a few times.

If you're invited to a yaqona (kava) drinking session, remember that seating is governed by seniority and rank, so just sit where you're asked to. In particular, don't go and sit in front of the tānoa (kava bowl) unless you're invited to do so.

FIJIAN

SAME TO YOU

To express appreciation of the opposite sex and inquire into the possibility of further acquaintance, a common expression is uro. This word originally meant 'fat', and, by extension, 'delicious'. If you want to respond or carry on the joke, say bā rewa gā vei iko or i keri gā, meaning 'same to you'.

FIJIAN

THE YAQONA RITUAL

A daily yaqona-drinking ritual was an integral part of the old Fijian religion, and only chiefs, priests and important male elders took part.

Yaqona is still central to Fijian culture and is ritually served on important occasions. Remote villages still practise quasi-religious ceremonies around the kava bowl. Even informal drinking still involves a fair amount of ritual.

Yaqona is served in rounds. When you're offered a bowl of yaqona, clap with cupped hands (cobo) two or three times, take the cup and drink its contents in one go. Return the cup and cobo again. After others have drunk you may cobo and/or say maca! (the cup is empty). If you're among friends and feel it's time for the next round, say taki or talo. If your cup comes and you want to stop drinking, say au sā kua mada or au sā cegu mada and put your palm out in front of you in a 'stop' gesture. If you want to stretch your legs, you can request permission by saying au se dodo mada

Family

Most indigenous Fijians live in villages in mataqali (extended family groups) and acknowledge a hereditary chief (tūraga) who is usually male. Clans gather for deaths and marriages, to celebrate vakatawase (New Year, see page 39) and to renew ties with other clans. Such gatherings, called sōlevu, include lovo feasts (where food is cooked in a pit oven), mekes (traditional dances) and ceremonial exchanges of food and valuables.

All the words below are listed in the first person possessive (my aunt, my brother, and so on).

my ...

aunt (father's sister)	noqu nei
aunt (mother's older sister)	tinaqu levu; noqu nā levu
aunt (mother's younger sister)	tinaqu lailai; noqu nā lailai

brother (female speaking)	gānequ
older brother (male speaking)	tuakaqu
younger brother (male speaking)	taciqu
children	luvequ
daughter	luvequ (yalewa)
daughter-in-law	vugoqu (yalewa)
family	iratou na wekaqu
father	tamaqu; noqu tā
father-in-law	noqu mōmō; vugoqu
grandfather	tukaqu
grandmother	buqu; noqu būbū
husband	watiqu
husband and children	noqu veitamani
mother	tinaqu; noqu nā
mother-in-law	noqu nei; vugoqu
relative	wekaqu
sister (male speaking)	gānequ
older sister (female speaking)	tuakaqu
younger sister (female speaking)	taciqu

FIJIAN

BROTHER, SISTER, COUSIN

If a cousin is the child of your father's brother or mother's sister, he or she is considered your brother or sister, otherwise:

cousin (male's male cousin)	tavalequ
cousin (female's female cousin)	dauvequ/raivaqu
cousin (of the opposite sex)	tavalequ/davolaqu

son	luvequ (tagane)
son-in-law	vugoqu (tagane)
uncle (father's older brother)	tamaqu levu; noqu tā levu
uncle (father's younger brother)	tamaqu lailai; noqu tā lailai
uncle (mother's brother)	noqu mōmō; vugoqu
wife	watiqu
wife and children	noqu veitinani

FIJIAN

Staying with a Family

Such is the hospitality of Fijians that even a chance acquaintance may lead to your being invited to stay with a family.

Should you be fortunate enough for this to happen, prepare yourself for a novel and heartwarming experience. Fijians are masters at entertaining, and go out of their way to make guests feel as comfortable as possible. You'll probably be given the best room in the house (or, if in a village, the only bed), and served with the best foods within your hosts' means.

When you arrive, bring some yaqona (kava) with you. This is for your isevusevu (a formal presentation comparable to bringing a bottle of wine when you visit). In towns, it's acceptable to bring a few bags of pounded yaqona (taga yaqona), which is available in small shops, some markets, service stations and many private houses. For a more classy entrance, buy a bundle of waka (kava roots), available at markets and some shops and service stations.

'FIJIANISE' YOUR NAME

If you'd like to 'Fijianise' your name, here are some of the most common equivalents:

John	Jone	Mary	Mere
Peter	Pita	Jane	Seini
Paul	Paula	Elizabeth	Ilisāpeci
Timothy	Tīmoci	Margaret	Makareta

ground yaqona (inferior but cheap)	yaqona qaqi
pounded yaqona	yaqona tuki
a bundle of yaqona root	dua na ivesu waka

Soon after arriving at the house, tell your host that you'd like to sevusevu, saying Dua na yaqona lailai au kauta mai, 'I've bought a little yaqona'.

You won't, of course, be expected to actually present it yourself. In a village, your host may accept, or take you to the valelevu (chief's house) for it to be presented to the local tūraga (chief). When you're about to leave, you should present another yaqona as your itatau (farewell offering).

The dictates of Fijian hospitality require that you be looked after as long as you stay. Nobody will tell you to leave, nor will anybody ask you to contribute to the household. But to be fair, you should make a regular contribution, in cash or, preferably, store goods. Hand them quietly to the woman of the house, saying something like Dua noqu kā ni veivuke lailai 'Just a little help from me'. When you're about to leave, give some small presents for them to remember you by. If you'd like to give cash, you might say it's for the kids' school fees (icurucuru ni vuli) or to buy sugar (ivoli ni suka). Your gift will be accepted with a short expression of thanks and clapping (cobo).

FIJIAN

DID YOU KNOW ...	Traditional Fijian homes are rectangular structures with hipped or gabled roofs. Pandanus mats cover a packed-earth floor and there's often a sleeping compartment at one end behind a curtain. Traditional house building is a skilled trade passed from father to son. The only village remaining where every home is traditional is Navala, in the highlands of Vitilevu.

FOOD

If eating sweets, biscuits, fruit or snacks, or smoking cigarettes, just hand over the packet or bunch of bananas or whatever, perhaps saying qori, 'there you are'. To say something like 'you can have one' is considered ridiculously mean – even asking Kana? or Dua na kemu?, 'Would you like one?' might suggest you are reluctant to share.

If you see someone while you're eating, it's customary to invite them to eat with you. Use an appropriate gesture or call. The bare minimum is to point at the food and look inquiringly. In increasing order of politeness, use (mai) kana, (mai) kana mada or nī (mai) kana mada. The word mai means 'come and', so is more appropriate when calling to someone some distance away. To all who pass when people are drinking kava, it's customary to call Mai dua na bilo! 'Come and have a cup!'.

To decline such an invitation, use a word of thanks such as vinaka, and say or point to where you're going. In familiar situations, the minimum is to cock the head, meaning 'no thanks', and pat the stomach to show it's full.

Grace is always said before meals. During meals, the host may say:

Kana vakavinaka.	Eat heartily.
Kana vakalevu.	Eat a lot.
O(nī) kana vakalailai!	You're eating too little!

When you've had enough, say:

Thanks a lot for the food, may I retire?	Vinaka vakalevu na kākana, au kere vakacegu.
I've had enough, thanks very much.	Au sā mamau, vinaka vakalevu.

A typical Fijian meal consists of two components – a boiled or earth-oven baked root vegetable, and what is called the icoi, fish or meat and/or a green vegetable.

FIJIAN

Roadside and market vendors sell all kinds of fresh fruit and snacks such as silā (boiled maize/corn), dovu (sugar cane), pinati (peanuts) and bini (spiced peas, originally an Indian food).

When something is cooked in coconut cream, it's said to be vakalolo (not to be confused with the same word, vakalolo, meaning a kind of sweet pudding). When baked in an earth-oven, it's said to be vavi. Fried is tavuteke. When a dish is served with fermented coconut, kora, it's said to be vākora

Local Dishes

The following is a small selection of local icoi you're likely to encounter.

ika vakalolo
  fish boiled in coconut cream, often served with a green vegetable. Fish is served whole and the head is the most highly esteemed part.

kokoda
  marinated raw fish or shellfish (actually more popular among tourists than Fijians)

kuita vakalolo
  octopus stewed in coconut cream

lairo vakasoso
  lairo (landcrab) meat stuffed in the shell with coconut cream and chopped onions

palusami
  corned beef and coconut cream wrapped in rourou (taro leaves) and baked in the earth-oven

vuaka vavi
  pork baked whole in the earth-oven

Green Vegetables

bele
  also known as 'island cabbage', but in Fiji it's invariably called by its Fijian name

FIJIAN

FIJIAN

duruka
  called 'Fiji asparagus' but actually related to sugarcane

lumi
  seaweed

moca or tubua
  a kind of spinach

ota
  fern leaves

rourou
  taro leaves

Root Vegetables & Other Staples

breadfruit	uto
cassava	tavioka
cooking banana	vudi
sweet potato	kumala
taro	dalo
wild yam	tikau/rauva/tīvoli
yam	uvi

Desserts

Fijian desserts are eaten at any time.

ivi
  boiled Tahitian chestnuts, usually wrapped in a kind of taro-leaf parcel

ōtai
  Fijian fruit salad, consisting of grated unripe mango sweetened with sugar and served with grated coconut

vakalolo
  any of a number of Fijian puddings which are essentially baked and pounded vegetable root served in a syrup or with grated coconut

vudi vakasoso
  ripe cooking banana served in thick coconut cream with grated coconut

GETTING AROUND

Fijians are usually happy to help a stranger, so don't be shy about asking. At the same time, remember that part of Fiji's charm is its informality, and while there are such things as bus and ship timetables, they tend not to be taken very seriously and people don't get too upset when things don't run according to schedule.

Directions

When giving directions, the most common reference points are trees and hedges.

by the ...	i na ...
breadfruit tree	vuniuto
coconut tree	vuniniu
hibiscus hedge	bā senitoa
mango tree	vunimaqo
rain tree	vunivaivai

FIJIAN

Compass bearings are never used. Instead you'll hear:

on the land side of ...	mai ... i vanua
on the sea side of ...	mai ... i wai
the far side of ...	mai ... (yani) i liu
this side of ...	mai ... i muri

Bus

Local buses are one of the wonders of Fiji, very cheap and a lot of fun. There are designated bus stops, but in the country you can wave down a bus practically anywhere. Although buses have route numbers, people usually refer to the places they go to (basi ni Nasēsē, 'Nasēsē bus'; basi ni valenibula, 'hospital bus').

Bus timetables are generally closely guarded secrets, and often known to drivers only vaguely if at all. On the other hand, in most towns buses are frequent.

It is the custom in Fiji for men to give up their seats to women and the elderly. If you have an aisle seat, it's impolite to reach in front of the person beside you to pull the cord, so attract their attention (by tapping or scratching a couple of times on their thigh) and point to the cord. If you can't get their attention in time, then reach for the cord saying jilou. If you have a window seat, say au lako mada yani to go past your fellow passenger, and likewise if there are standing passengers when you're getting off, saying jilou as you squeeze through.

Car

Road signs and driving courtesies are pretty standard if not rigorously observed. Even on the main highway, always be prepared for the unexpected, such as wandering livestock and young men pounding kava on the road. Two customs in particular might be unfamiliar. The signal to a following driver that the road ahead is clear to overtake is to activate the right indicator. This means that if you're following a vehicle and the right indicator flashes, it may mean either 'please overtake, the road ahead is clear' or 'I'm about to turn right, so if you attempt to overtake me there'll be a collision'. Best to stay put.

FIJIAN

Another is that all traffic stops as a sign of respect when a funeral cortege comes from the opposite direction. The lead car of the procession usually has its headlights on, so there may be some warning, but often the first thing you know is when the car ahead of you comes to a sudden halt for no apparent reason.

In the Country

It's important to realise that in Fiji, even the most desolate-looking areas and the densest forests have owners who have a profound, almost mystical, attachment to their land. By all means explore, picnic, swim in the river and so on, but leave the place as you found it. To camp, you should seek permission, and present yaqona as an isevusevu (gift on arrival) and itatau (farewell offering). Places with a high concentration of culti-vated plants (such as coconuts or mangoes) are probably old villages, and should be avoided. Likewise places with stands of red-leaved plants such as crotons and cordyline, which are probably burial grounds. Many caves are also old burial places.

If you'd like to look around a village, don't just walk straight in. Talk to someone and say Au sarasara mada e loma ni koro 'I'd like to look around the village' and they'll be happy to show you around.

FIJIAN

CONTEMPORARY MUSIC

Contemporary local music is very popular in Fiji. A typical Fijian band consists of two or three lead singers – often men singing falsetto – who harmonise, and a large number of bass singers accompanied by acoustic guitars, a ukelele and sometimes a mandolin. Like the chanters in a meke (traditional dance), they prefer to sit huddled in a group facing inwards. More western-style groups such as Sakiusa Bulicokocoko, Laisa Vulakoro and Seru Serevi are also popular in other Pacific islands.

CAMPING OUT

Camping is very rare in Fiji. The natural reaction of a Fijian to a camper is to feel great pity and insist on bringing them home to a decent house. Keep in mind that it's prohibited to camp on village land without permission.

FIJIAN

Geographical Terms

agriculture	teitei
bay	toba
beach	matāsawa
bridge	wavu
cave	qaravatu
city	siti
earthquake	uneune
farm	iteitei
forest	veikau
grassland	veicō; (reed-covered) talāsiga
harbour	ikelekele ni waqa
headland	ucuna
hill	delana
hot spring	waikatakata
island	yanuyanu
jungle	veikauloa
lake	drano
landslide	sisi na qele; loka
mountain	ulunivanua
mountain range	veidelana
ocean	wasawasa
pool (for swimming)	tobunisili
reef	cakau
river	uciwai
village	koro
waterfall	savu

Seasons

autumn	vulaimatumatua
spring	vulaitubutubu
summer	vulaikatakata
winter	vulaililiwa
dry season	vulaisiga
rainy season	vulaiuca
hurricane season	vulaicagilaba

Souvenirs & Artefacts

bark cloth	masi
club	iwau
earrings	sau
garland	salusalu
grass skirt	liku vau
handicraft	cakacaka ni liga
kava bowl	tānoa
mask	matavulo
mats	ibe
necklace	itaube
pottery	tulituli
ring	mama
shells	qānivivili
wood carvings	sivisivi

FIJIAN

FESTIVALS

There are many festivals in Fiji, reflecting the varied ethnic and religious make-up of the country. For Fijians, Christmas and Easter are celebrated, but essentially as religious festivals.

Vakatawase

the major secular festival, the celebration for the New Year, begins at midnight on 1 January and goes on until the village chief declares it tabu 'forbidden', usually a week or so before the new school year begins. In stark contrast to the usual custom in villages, you can make as much noise as you like during vakatawase, and children love staying up late (sometimes all night) walking around in groups, singing songs and letting out whoops, playing riotous games of hide-and-seek, letting off fireworks and detonating bamboo cannon, and beating the hell out of the village lali (hollowed-out log drum), which is at other times is strictly forbidden. It's becoming increasingly popular in towns too. A custom peculiar to Vakatawase is veisui (throwing water at each

> ## BY THE HOUR
>
> A note of caution – the term 'guesthouse' and its Fijian equivalent bure ni vūlagi often refer to establishments offering rooms for hire by the hour. The word motel sometimes has the same connotation.

other). Children and young people do it just for fun, but adults are more cautious, since custom demands that they compensate the 'dunkee' by giving them an article of clothing as a ivakamāmaca (something to dry themselves with).

Sōlevu

Fijians hold large gatherings called sōlevu or oga for occasions such as funerals and marriages. At some, you might have the good fortune to see meke (traditional dances) performed. Show your appreciation by shouting vinaka and giving fakawela (gifts) – either give dancers, while they're performing, small gifts such as sweets, chewing gum, lengths of printed cloth, or dollar notes, or sprinkle talcum powder or waiwai (scented coconut oil) on them.

Adi

in towns, Fijians often have fund-raising festivals called Adi, in which they sell produce, food and handicrafts and where meke (traditional dances) are also performed

If you go to a village, you might be invited to a simple gunu yaqona (kava party) or a taralalā, an old-style European-type dance with a small local guitar band, where the women usually have to drag the men to the floor. There might be fund-raising functions such as a kati (buying playing cards and winning small 'prizes', usually food items, if your card is cut from the pack) or gunusede, a riotous affair with much joking where you not only pay for your own kava,

AGELESS TABOO

Age isn't a taboo subject in Fiji, so don't be surprised or offended if people ask your age. Birthdays aren't normally celebrated, and quite a few Fijians neither know nor care on what day they were born.

but pay to have full cups served to others in friendly rivalry. If someone buys you a drink and you don't want it, you can bid a higher price for someone else to drink it.

TIME & DATES
Telling the Time

When expressing minutes past the hour, Fijians use the following phrasing:

A minutes past B   sivi na B ina A (na miniti)

The order for minutes before the hour is as in English.

A minutes to B   vō e A (na miniti) me B

(See page 42 for numbers.)

sunrise	cabe na siga
dawn	mataka lailai
morning (until about 10 am)	mataka
midday/afternoon (10 am to 3 pm)	sigalevu
noon	sigalevu tūtū
evening	yakavi
twilight	karobo
sundown	dromu na siga
midnight	bogilevu tūtū

FIJIAN

FIJIAN

Days

Sunday	Sigatabu
Monday	Mōniti
Tuesday	Tūsiti
Wednesday	Vukelulu
Thursday	Lotulevu
Friday	Vakaraubuka
Saturday	Vakarauwai

Months

January	Jānueri
February	Feperueri
March	Maji
April	Epereli
May	Mē
June	Junē
July	Julai
August	Okosita
September	Sepiteba
October	Okotova
November	Nōveba
December	Tīseba

NUMBERS

0	saiva
1	dua
2	rua
3	tolu
4	vā
5	lima
6	ono
7	vitu
8	walu
9	ciwa
10	tini

11	tínikadua
12	tínikarua
13	tínikatolu
14	tínikavā
15	tínikalima
16	tínikaono
17	tínikavitu
18	tínikawalu
19	tínikaciwa
20	rúasagavulu
21	rúasagavulukadua
22	rúasagavulukarua
30	tólusagavulu
31	tólusagavulukadua
40	vāsagavulu
50	límasagavulu
60	ónosagavulu
70	vítusagavulu
80	wálusagavulu
90	cíwasagavulu
100	dua na drau
101	dua na drau ka dua
102	dua na drau ka rua
193	dua na drau cíwasagavulukatolu
200	rua na drau
300	tolu na drau
400	vā na drau
500	lima na drau
600	ono na drau
700	vitu na drau
800	walu na drau
900	ciwa na drau
1000	dua na udolu
2000	rua na udolu
100,000	dua na drau na udolu
one million	dua na milioni
two million	rua na milioni

FIJIAN

FIJIAN

INITIATION CEREMONIES

Girls' initiation into adulthood, the veiqia rite, which was practised in some regions into the 1930s, involved elaborate tattooing of the pubic area. Girls were told that it would enhance their beauty and sex drive.

Each village had a female daubati (hereditary tattoo specialist) to perform the procedure. It was extremely painful, and could take up to a year to complete. A mixture of soot and oil was tapped into the skin with with a spiked pick and light mallet. A celebratory feast was held after the procedure was complete, and the young woman was then entitled to wear the liku (skirt of womanhood) and to marry.

Boys' initiaion ceremonies involved ritual circumcision. Afterward, a boy was entitled to wear the loincloth of manhood, grow his hair and move to the men's hut. Circumcision is still an important occasion for a boy and his family, as is the subsequent feast for friends and relatives.

HEALTH

All health workers speak English, but if you want to try the Fijian herbal medicine or massage, you may need to explain your symptoms in Fijian.

Ailments

I'm sick.	Au tauvimate.
I've been bitten by something.	Au sā laukata.
I feel weak.	Au malummalumu.
I've been vomiting.	Au lualua.
I can't sleep.	Au sega ni moce rawa.
It hurts here.	E mosi i kē.

SONG: ISALEI

Isalei is a Fijian farewell song played for travellers.

Isaisa, vulagi lasa dina
  Isaisa, most welcome guest
Nomu lako au na rarawa kina
  Your leaving will make me sad
Cava beka ko a mai cakava
  Whatever you came here to do
Nomu lako au na sega ni lasa
  I'll miss you when you've gone

Isalei, na noqu rarawa
  Isalei, I'm so unhappy
Ni ko sa na vodo e na mataka
  That you're leaving in the morning
Bau nanuma na nodatou lasa
  Remember our happiness
Mai Viti, nanuma tiko ga
  In Fiji, always remember

Vanua rogo na nomuni vanua
  Your land is a famous land
Kena ca ni levu tu na ua
  With turbulent waters
Lomaqu voli meu bau butuka
  I have a yearning to visit it
Tovolea ke balavu na bula
  I'll try, if I live long enough

Domoni dina na nomu yanuyanu
  Your island is truly beautiful
Kena kau wale na salusalu
  Its plants all scented garlands
Mocelolo, bua na kukuwalu
  Mocelolo, bua and kukuwalu,
Lagakali, maba na rosidamu
  Lagakali, maba and red roses

FIJIAN

I have (a/an) ...

cold	Au tauvi matetaka.
cough	Au vūvū.
diarrhoea	Au coka.
headache	E mosi na uluqu.
itch	Au milamila.
rheumatism	Au tauvi sasala.
sore throat	E mosi noqu itilotilo.
sunburn	Au katīsiga.
swollen ...	E vuce na ... qu.
temperature	Au katakata.

FIJIAN

HAWAIIAN

HAWAIIAN ISLANDS

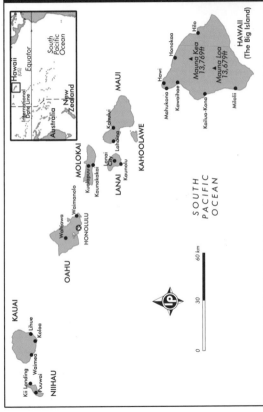

HAWAIIAN

INTRODUCTION

Hawaii is at the northern apex of the cultural area known as the Polynesian Triangle, which extends south-west to New Zealand and south-east to Easter Island. The languages spoken within this area, including Samoan, Tongan, Tahitian, Rapanui and Maori, to name a few, belong to the Polynesian language family, a part of the Austronesian language family. This group includes languages such as Malagasy, which is spoken as far away as Madagascar. Settled some 1500 years ago by Polynesians from the central Pacific, Hawaii was isolated from the west until the arrival of Captain Cook in 1778.

In 1820, missionaries arrived in Hawaii, and in an effort to spread Christianity, began teaching Hawaiians to read and write. Through time, the Hawaiian language was replaced by English as the commonly spoken language in Hawaii. In 1896, Hawaiian was banned as the medium of instruction in Hawaii's public schools, which led to the further decline of the language.

Many Hawaiian families had lost their mother tongue for several generations before the interest in the language began to reappear. In the 1970s and 1980s, a resurgence of interest in Hawaiian culture, history and language began. In 1978, Hawaiian was made an official language of the State of Hawaii, along with English. In the 1980s, the Hawaiian language immersion movement began with total immersion pre-schools in the style of those established by the Maori in New Zealand. Total immersion grade, middle and secondary schools followed.

Although English is spoken everywhere in Hawaii, a visitor has a greater chance of hearing the Hawaiian language being spoken today than they would have had 20 or 30 years ago. Hawaiian used to be heard mainly among elders or in isolated communities, but today can be heard on the street, in shopping centres, hotels and playgrounds. Hawaiians are very proud of their language and are actively working to assure its survival.

PRONUNCIATION

A Hawaiian alphabet was established in 1826 and is very similar to
that of other Polynesian languages. Two basic rules of Hawaiian
spelling are that two or more consonants never appear next to
each other, and that every word ends with a vowel. Hawaiian isn't
difficult to pronounce, and your effort to pronounce it properly
will be appreciated.

Vowels

There are five vowels in the Hawaiian alphabet, which sound
similar to their English equivalents. Each vowel has both a short
and long pronunciation, and long vowels are indicated by placing
a macron over the vowel (ā, ē, ī, ō and ū).

a	as the 'a' in father
e	as the 'e' in egg
i	as the 'i' in ski
o	as the 'o' in home
u	as the 'ue' in blue

Consonants

Hawaiian has eight consonants – h, k, l, m, n, p, w and '. The
consonants are all familiar to the English speaker, except perhaps
the 'okina, or glottal stop ('). The use of the 'okina is crucial
because it can indicate a difference in meaning. The name Hawaii
itself is pronounced with a glottal stop in the Hawaiian language,
as Hawai'i. Native speakers don't use the 'okina when writing
because they know the meaning by context, but the second language learner will benefit by the inclusion of both macrons and
glottal stops.

w	like 'w' or like 'v'
'	glottal stop ('okina), like the sound between the words in 'uh-oh'

MEETING PEOPLE

Hawaiians are usually friendly and enjoy meeting people. The first Hawaiian word you hear is aloha (hello/welcome). You may be presented with a lei (garland), with or without a kiss. Although a kiss is not a traditional gesture, it has become common practice for people to embrace and exchange kisses on the cheek, especially if they're good friends or related to one another.

Greetings & Goodbyes

Hello.	Aloha.
Good morning.	Aloha kakahiaka.
Good day. (midday greeting)	Aloha awakea.
Good afternoon.	Aloha 'auinalā.
Good evening.	Aloha ahiahi.
Goodbye.	Aloha a hui hou.

Etiquette

Yes.	'Ae.
No.	'A'ole.
Please.	E 'olu'olu.
Thank you.	Mahalo.
Excuse me.	E kala mai ia'u.
Sorry.	E kala mai.
Please sit down.	E 'olu'olu e noho iho.
I understand.	Maopopo ia'u.
I don't understand.	'A'ole maopopo ia'u.
Correct.	Pololei.
Good.	Maika'i.
OK.	Hiki.
Never mind.	'A'ole pilikia.
No problem.	'A'ole pilikia.

HAWAIIAN

ALOHA

Aloha, the traditional Hawaiian greeting, can mean 'love', 'welcome' or 'goodbye'.

Body Language

When meeting someone or passing someone on the street, you might notice that they raise their eyebrows at you. Don't be alarmed, it's an automatic non-verbal greeting found in Hawaii and elsewhere in the Pacific. Eye contact in Hawaii may be different than in other English-speaking countries. People, especially strangers, may briefly glance at you, then turn away. If you stare at a Hawaiian, they may interpret it as a challenge and ask you what you're looking at. This is in direct contradiction to Westerners' belief that honesty is shown by looking someone straight in the eye.

Family

The basic Hawaiian family unit is the ʻohana (extended family). Because genealogy is an important aspect of Hawaiian culture, Hawaiians take pride in being able to identify relationships. At times it can seem that most Hawaiians are related when just about everyone they introduce you to are relatives.

aunt	ʻanakē (from English)
brother (female speaking)	kaikunāne
child	keiki
children	kamaliʻi
cousin	hoahānau
daughter	kaikamahine
father	makua kāne
grandchild	moʻopuna
grandfather	kupuna kāne
grandma	tūtū/kūkū
grandmother	kupuna wahine
grandpa	tūtū/kūkū
husband/male	kāne
mother	makuahine
older sibling of the same sex	kaikuaʻana
sister (male speaking)	kaikuahine
son	keiki kāne
uncle	ʻanakala (from English)

wife/female	wahine
younger sibling of the same sex	kaikaina

People

Caucasian person	haole
commoners (of old Hawaii)	maka'āinana
dentist	kauka niho
doctor	kauka
expert in any occupation in ancient Hawaii	kahuna
friend	hoaaloha
group/organisation	hui
indigenous Hawaiian	kanaka maoli
man	kāne
native-born person or long-time resident	kama'āina (lit: child of the land)
part-white (person or song)	hapa haole
person	kanaka
person of mixed blood	hapa
royalty/chief	ali'i
student	haumana
teacher	kumu
visitor/newcomer	malihini
woman	wahine

Gods, Goddesses & Other Deities

akua
> major Hawaiian god. When capitalised, Akua usually refers to the Christian god.

'aumakua
> ancestral guardian gods which take animal forms such as sharks (manō), owls (pueo) and eels (puhi)

Hi'iakaikapoliopele
> Pele's favourite younger sister

HAWAIIAN

Hina
  Polynesian goddess (wife of Kū, one of the four main gods)

Ka'ahupahau
  benevolent shark goddess of Pu'uloa (Pearl Harbor)

Kamapua'a
  demigod, half man-half pig. Rival and lover of Pele.

Kanaloa
  god of the oceans; winds

Kāne
  god of creation; life

Kū
  god of war

Laka
  patron deity of the hula

Lono
  god of agriculture

MONGOOSE

While visiting Hawaii, you might catch a quick glimpse of a little brown, weasel-like creature dashing across the road and disappearing into the brush. It's the mongoose, a native of India that was brought to Hawaii by the sugar growers to help with the battle against rats. The only problem was that the rat is nocturnal and the mongoose is diurnal, thus they each did their own thing at different times of the day. The mongoose has no natural predator in Hawaii, so its population has grown virtually unchecked. It has caused problems for farmers because the mongoose loves eggs and young fowl. On occasion, you might see them at rural visitor stops running to retrieve bits of leftover food.

Māui
> pan-Polynesian demigod who performed feats to improve the quality of life of his people. He raised the sky so that his mother's kapa (bark cloth) could dry, and fished the islands out of the ocean when his fishhook snagged the ocean floor and he tugged with such force that the islands of Hawaii were yanked to the surface. They would have been one mass except that someone looked back and the line snapped.

menehune
> a people believed to perform miraculous feats overnight, always evading capture. According to legend, they built many of Hawaii's fishponds, heiau and other stonework.

Papa
> earth mother

Pele
> goddess of fire; volcano. There are several proverbs that link Puna, the easternmost point of the Big Island, with Pele. To express anger, someone might say Ke lauahi maila o Pele ia Puna, 'Pele is pouring lava out on Puna'.

Wākea
> sky father

FOOD
The Lū'au

Food and eating have a special significance in Hawaiian culture. Many activities culminate in a lū'au or feast (formerly called pā'ina or 'aha'aina). A child's first birthday, a wedding or a graduation all warrant a celebration. Getting together to prepare food for any occasion is a time for family and friends to help each other, catch up on the latest news and just enjoy each other's company. You'll have many opportunities to attend commercial lū'au, which are modified for the non-Hawaiian palate. However, if you do have a chance to attend a private lū'au, by all means go for it – it'll be a very pleasant experience. Hawaiians cook food in a variety of ways and especially enjoy delicacies from the ocean.

Traditional Cooking Methods

hākui	steamed in a container with a little water and hot rocks
kālua	cooked in an imu (underground oven)
kōʻala	meat broiled over hot embers
lāwalu	fish or meat wrapped in ti leaves and cooked over hot embers
pūholo	meat cooked by stuffing it with hot rocks and then wrapping it to retain the heat
pūlehu	vegetables and nuts, such as ʻuala (sweet potato), ʻulu (breadfruit) and kukui (nuts), roasted in hot embers

Local Foods

haupia	pia (arrowroot or cornstarch) and coconut cream pudding
heʻe lūʻau	octopus with lūʻau and coconut cream, called squid lūʻau
iʻa maka	seasoned raw fish
ʻinamona	a condiment made from the roasted Kukui nut kernel
kalo	taro corm
kāmano i lomi ʻia	salt salmon, minced – traditionally kneaded (lomilomi) – with tomatoes and onions. Often called lomilomi salmon
kōʻele pālau	mashed cooked sweet potato mixed with coconut cream
kūlolo	cooked grated kalo and coconut cream pudding
laulau	cooked bundles of pork and fish wrapped in lūʻau and ti leaves
limu	seaweed
lūʻau	young kalo leaves used as a green vegetable
nīoi	little hot chili peppers
pāpaʻi	seasoned raw crab
paʻakai	sea salt

pia	beer
poi	mashed kalo mixed with water. Main Hawaiian staple.
poke	raw fish cut into cubes and then seasoned
pua'a kālua	pork cooked in an imu, (underground oven). Commonly called kālua pig.
wai halakahiki	pineapple juice
wai hua'ai	fruit juice
wai kuawa	guava juice
wai liliko'i	passion fruit juice
wai momona	punch
wana me ka 'ula	sea urchin with lobster
'ōpae	small mountain shrimp
'opihi	limpets
'uala	sweet potato
'ulu	breadfruit

GETTING AROUND
Geographical Terms

ahupua'a	land division from the upland to the sea
'āina	land
ala	pathway
hana/hono	bay
heiau	ancient Hawaiian place of worship
honua	earth
i kai	to head toward the sea
i uka	to head inland
kai	sea/saltwater

HAWAIIAN

DIRECTIONS

When asking for directions in Hawaii, you'll notice that cardinal compass directions (such as north and south-east) aren't always used. Instead, you may be directed with reference to a geographic feature or landmark.

ko'a	fishing shrine
ko'olau	windward side of an island
kona	leeward side of an island
Kū'ula	fishing god
luakini	type of heiau dedicated to the war god Kū and used for human sacrifices
ma kai	seaward
ma uka	inland
mauna	mountain
moana	ocean
moku	land district; island
pali	cliff
puna	spring
pu'u	hill
pu'uhonua	place of refuge
wai	freshwater

Placenames

Hawaiian placenames are often descriptions of the geographic feature they represent, or are references to historical events. The descriptive words or adjectives follow the nouns they modify, for instance Mauna Kea is 'white mountain', Punahou is 'new spring' and Ala Moana is 'ocean pathway'.

Ala Wai	freshwater canal or waterway
Haleakalā	house of the sun
Halekūlani	house befitting royalty (hotel)

HAWAIIAN SIGNS

Kapu, meaning 'taboo', is part of the ancient Hawaiian social system. Today, the word's often seen on signs meaning 'Keep Out'.

The word kōkua means 'help and cooperation'. Please Kokua written on rubbish bins is the equivalent to 'Don't litter'.

HAWAIIAN

Halemaʻumaʻu	fern house
Haleʻiwa	house of the frigate bird
Hanalei	crescent bay
Honolulu	protected bay
Kailua	two seas
Kāneʻohe	bamboo man
Kealakekua	pathway of the god
Keauhou	the new era/current
Keawaʻula	the red harbour
Keʻanae	the mullet
Lahaina	cruel sun (said to be named for droughts)
Mauna Loa	long mountain
Maunahuʻihuʻi	chilly mountain
Maunaʻala	fragrant mountain
Puʻukapu	sacred hill
Puʻukoholā	whale hill (heiau near Kawaihae, Hawaii island)
Puʻuloa	long hill
Waikīkī	spurting water
Waimānalo	drinking water
Waimea	reddish water (as from erosion of red soil)
Waiʻanae	mullet water

Street Names

Like placenames, street names reflect Hawaiian culture and history. Many streets are named for people who have featured in Hawaiian history.

Kaimana Hila	Diamond Head (lit: Diamond Hill)
Kalākaua	Hawaii's last king (main street through Waikīkī)

HAWAIIAN

NEIGHBOR ISLANDS

The Neighbor Islands is a term used to refer to the main Hawaiian islands outside of Oahu.

Kalaniana'ole	nephew of Kapi'olani, a delegate to Congress
Kamehameha	king who united all the islands except Kaua'i
Kapi'olani	Kalākaua's queen
Ka'ahumanu	Kamehameha's favourite wife
Ka'iulani	niece of Kalākaua and Lili'uokalani
Ke'eaumoku	an ali'i (chief) during the reign of Kamehameha I; Kamehameha's father in law
Kūhiō	another name for Kalaniana'ole
Lē'ahi	old name for Kaimana Hila (Diamond Hill)
Likelike	mother of Ka'iulani; sister of the last king and queen
Lili'uokalani	Hawaii's last queen (Kalākaua's sister)

Animals

ant	naonao
bat	'ōpe'ape'a
bird	manu
butterfly	pulelehua
cat	pōpoki
cattle	pipi
centipede	kanapī
chicken	moa
cockroach	'elelū
dog	'īlio
dolphin	nai'a
donkey	kēkake/'ēkake
duck	kakā
eel	puhi
fish	i'a
flea	'uku
gecko	mo'o

geese	nēnē
goat	kao
hawk	ʻio
horse	lio
insect	mea kolo
lice	ʻuku
mongoose	ʻiole manakuke
mosquito	makika
owl	pueo
pig	puaʻa
porpoise	nuʻao
rat	ʻiole
scorpion	moʻonihoʻawa
sea cucumber	loli
seal	ʻīlio holo i ka uaua
shark	manō
spider	lanalana
starfish	peʻa
turtle	honu
whale	koholā

Plants & Flowers

birdnest fern	ʻēkaha
candlenut	kukui
carnation	ponimōʻī
cigar flower	kīkā
coconut	niu
crown flower	pua kalaunu
ginger	ʻawapuhi
hibiscus	pua aloalo
jasmine	pīkake
maidenhair fern	ʻiwaʻiwa
pandanus	hala
paper mulberry	wauke
plumeria/frangipani	pua melia
rose	loke

In the Surf

To Hawaiians, the ocean is a source of food and entertainment. Surfing and canoeing are favourite pastimes for people of all ages. Experienced surfers make surfboarding look so easy, but novices should beware – waves are very powerful and caution should be taken even when you're standing on the beach.

beach	kahakai
bodysurfing	kaha nalu; he'e umauma
canoe	wa'a
outrigger	ama
paddle	hoe
reef	papa
sand	one
surfboard	papa he'enalu
surfboarding	he'enalu
wave	nalu

HAWAIIAN

Souvenirs & Artefacts

holokū	long dress similar to the muʻumuʻu but more fitted
kiʻi	statue
lei	garlands made of flowers, leaves, shells or seeds
lei hulu	feather lei
lei pūpū	shell lei
muʻumuʻu	long or short Hawaiian dress
papa heʻenalu	surfboard
pāpale lauhala	lauhala (pandanus leaf) hat
ʻukulele	stringed musical instrument introduced by the Portuguese

HOLIDAYS & FESTIVALS

Aloha Festivals

> celebration of Hawaiian culture with parades, contests, canoe races and Hawaiian music. Festivities take place in September and October on every island.

Kamehameha Hula Competition

> one of Hawaii's biggest hula contests held in Honolulu near the end of June

Ka Molokai Makahiki

> modern-day version of the ancient makahiki festival. Celebrations include traditional Hawaiian games and sports, a fishing contest and Hawaiian music and hula. Held in Kaunakakai, Molokai in mid January.

Lei Day

> May Day (1 May) is Lei Day, celebrated with a lei-making competition

King Kamehameha Day

> on 11 June or the nearest weekend the statue of Kamehameha is decorated with long lei, and a parade is held through Waikīkī, ending at Kapiʻolani Park where Hawaiian crafts are usually demonstrated

Merrie Monarch Hula Festival
Hawaii's longest running hula competition is held in Hilo, on the weekend after Easter

Molokai Ka Hula Piko
held in Molokai in mid-May. Celebrates the birth of hula, with traditional dance performances, Hawaiian food and visits to sacred sites.

Prince Kūhiō Day
26 March, birthday of Prince Jonah Kūhiō Kalaniana'ole

Prince Lot Hula Festival
hula exhibition held in July at Oahu's Moanalua Gardens

Some festivals include colourful parades with fresh floral floats and women in flowing pā'ū (culottes) on horseback. Pā'ū riders wear colors and flowers according to the islands they represent.

ISLAND	FLOWER	COLOUR
Hawai'i	lehua	red
Maui	lokelani	pink
O'ahu	'ilima	yellow
Kaua'i	mokihana	purple
Moloka'i	kukui	green
Lāna'i	kauna'oa	orange
Ni'ihau	pūpū (shells)	white
Kaho'olawe	hinahina	gray

LETTER WRITING

Dear Sir/Madam	Aloha kāua
Humbly yours	'O au iho nō me ka ha'aha'a
Sincerely; Yours truly	'O au iho nō
With love	Me ke aloha
With warmest regards	Me ke aloha pumehana
With never-ending love	Me ke aloha pau'ole

HAWAIIAN

THE HULA

Hula is the traditional dance of Hawaii. The hula is taught in hālau or hālau hula, which means school or dance school. In ancient Hawaii, the hula accompanied oli (chanting). Today, that style has been joined by a new style of hula that accompanies contemporary Western-style music. When watching the hula, remember to try to keep your eyes on the dancers' hands because the hands tell the story of the chant or song. There are many hālau hula and they often enter competitions to see who are the best at their craft. Here are some words you'll hear in the hula, but remember the hands tell the story.

Body Terms

'ā'ī	neck
ihu	nose
kīkala	hips
kino	body
lehelehe	lips
lima	hands
maka	eyes
papālina	cheeks
poli	breast
po'o	head
pu'uwai	heart
waha	mouth
wāwae	legs/feet

Things in Nature

'a'ala/onaona	fragrant
'aekai	beach
ānuenue	rainbow
i'a	fish
kahakai	beach
kai	sea
kaulana	fame/famous
kuahiwi	mountain
kumu	trees

HAWAIIAN

lā	sun
lei	garland
mahina	moon
makani	wind
manu	birds
moana	ocean
nalu	waves
nani	beauty
(kumu) niu	coconut (trees)
noe	mist
onaona	fragrant
one	sand
pali	cliffs
pua	flowers

HAWAIIAN NATIONAL ANTHEM

Hawai'i Pono'ī or Hawaii's Own is the Hawaiian National Anthem, written by King David Kalākaua.

Hawai'i Pono'ī
  Hawaii's own
Nānā i kou Mō'ī
  Look to your King
Ka lani ali'i, ke ali'i
  The royal chief
Makua lani e
  Royal Father
Kamehameha e
  Kamehameha
Na kāua e pale
  We shall defend
Me ka ihe
  With spears

punawai	spring (as of water)
ua	rain
uē	to cry
u'i	beauty
wailele	waterfall
waimaka	tears

Hula Instruments

'ili'ili	water-worn pebbles
ipu	gourd drum
ipu heke	double gourd drum

SONG: HAWAI'I ALOHA

Hawai'i Aloha or 'Beloved Hawai'i' is often sung at the close of Hawaiian gatherings.

E Hawai'i e ku'u one hānau e,
  O Hawaii, sands of my birth
Ku'u home, kulāiwi nei
  My native home
'Oli. nō au i nā pono lani ou
  I rejoice in your heavenly blessing
E Hawai'i, aloha e
  O Hawaii, aloha.

Chorus:
E hau'oli e nā 'ōpio o Hawai'i nei
  Happy are the youth of Hawaii
'Oli e, 'oli e
  Rejoice, rejoice
Mai nā aheahe makani e pā mai nei
  The gentle breezes blow
Mau ke aloha no Hawai'i.
  Forever I will love Hawaii.

HAWAIIAN

kālaʻau	sticks for dancing
pahu hula	hula drum
pūʻili	split bamboo rattle
ʻuliʻulī	feathered gourd rattle

Other Hula Terms

hālau hula	hula school
kīhei	shawl, tied at one shoulder
kuahu	altar for hālau hula
kumu hula	hula teacher
kūpeʻe	anklets/wristlets
lei hulu	feather garland
pāʻū	skirt

MYTHS & LEGENDS
The Legend of Breadfruit ('Ulu)

The god Kū walked among humans and fell in love with a Hawaiian woman, and together they raised a large family. He worked the land like any other mortal and no one knew of his true identity, not even his wife. There came a time when food became scarce and his wife and children were starving. He felt sorry for his family and told his wife that he could provide food for them, but that he'd have to go away and never return. At first the woman wouldn't hear of his leaving, but after hearing her children's cries of hunger, she consented to his plan.

They went into the yard and said their goodbyes, and then he stood on his head and started to disappear into the ground. He had instructed that the food would sprout from the spot where he entered the earth. His wife watched the spot every day and her tears watered it until a sprout appeared from which a tree grew so rapidly that in a few days the family had the food Kū had promised. The food was the ʻulu, the breadfruit, and was all the family needed to survive. Only the family was able to pick the ʻulu from this tree – if someone else tried, the tree would recede into the ground. After a while, sprouts grew from the parent tree which were then given to their neighbours for their gardens.

TIME & DATES

Traditionally, Hawaiians kept track of time using a lunar calendar – fishing and farming were planned according to the phases of the moon. Some still adhere to the lunar calendar, however, most now follow the Western calendar.

Days
Nā Lā o ka Pule

Monday	Pō'akahi
Tuesday	Pō'alua
Wednesday	Pō'akolu
Thursday	Pō'ahā
Friday	Pō'alima
Saturday	Pō'aono
Sunday	Lāpule

Months
Nā Mahina o ka Makahiki

January	'Ianuali
February	Pepeluali
March	Malaki
April	'Apelila
May	Mei
June	Iune
July	Iulai
August	'Aukake
September	Kepakemapa
October	'Okakopa
November	Nowemapa
December	Kēkēmapa

HAWAIIAN

SHAKA SIGN

Hawaiians greet each other with the shaka sign, made by extending the thumb and the little finger while holding the other fingers to the palm. The hand is then held out and shaken. This greeting is as common as waving.

NUMBERS

0	'ole	20	iwakālua
1	'ekahi	21	iwakāluakūmākahi
2	'elua	30	kanakolu
3	'ekolu	40	kanahā
4	'ehā	50	kanalima
5	'elima	60	kanaono
6	'eono	70	kanahiku
7	'ehiku	80	kanawalu
8	'ewalu	90	kanaiwa
9	'eiwa	100	haneli/hanele
10	'umi	101	ho'okahi haneli a me 'ekahi
11	'umikūmākahi	110	ho'okahi haneli a me 'umi
12	'umikūmālua	111	haneli a me 'umikūmākahi
13	'umikūmākolu	200	'elua haneli
14	'umikūmāhā	300	'ekolu haneli
15	'umikūmālima	1,000	kaukani
16	'umikūmāono	2,000	'elua kaukani
17	'umikūmāhiku	10,000	'umi kaukani
18	'umikūmāwalu	100,000	haneli kaukani
19	'umikūmāiwa	1,000,000	miliona

There is also a Hawaiian counting system based on four.

4	kāuna
40	ka'au
400	lau
4,000	mano
40,000	kini

KANAK LANGUAGES

NEW CALEDONIA

International
Date Line

Equator

New
Caledonia

Australia

New
Zealand

South
Pacific
Ocean

SOUTH
PACIFIC
OCEAN

Îles
Belep
• Waala

Astrolabe
Reefs

Poum •

• Pouébo

Beautemps-
Beaupré
Atoll

Koumac •

Ouvéa

Kaala-Gomen •

• Touho

Fayaoué •

• Koné   • Poindimié

CORAL
SEA

Lifou

• We

Tiga

• Poya

• Houaïlou

• Bourail

Tadin •

La Foa • • Thio

Maré

GRANDE
TERRE

• Bouloupari

• Païta
• Dumbéa

NOUMÉA

• Yaté

Amédée
Islet

Île Ouen

Île des
Pins

Vao •

0   50   100 km

THE KANAK LANGUAGES

INTRODUCTION

New Caledonia, or Kanaky as it's known to many indigenous inhabitants, lies in the south-west of the Pacific. Before France took possession in 1853, New Caledonia had contact with European sandalwood traders and whaling ships, who introduced new diseases which decimated the population.

Grande Terre, New Caledonia's main island, is around 400km long and 50km wide. In 1996 there were just under 188,000 inhabitants – 42% Melanesians, 37% Europeans, 12% Polynesians and the rest ethnic minorities such as Javanese and Vietnamese.

There are 28 distinct Kanak languages (not counting dialects), and all except one belong to the Melanesian branch of the Austronesian language family. The exception is Faga Uvea, spoken on Uvea, in the Loyalty Islands group, which is a Polynesian language. Kanak languages are extremely diverse, partly due to the succession of ancient peoples who inhabited the arc of Melanesia. This chapter will deal mainly with the most widely spoken Kanak language, Drehu, spoken in the Loyalty Islands.

Classification

During the colonial period, the distribution of languages was disturbed by the forced displacement of the population, during which enemy clans were arbitrarily grouped together. The languages of New Caledonia are divided into three main groups:

Northern Languages

Twelve languages are spoken in the north of New Caledonia. From north to south, they are Yâlayu, Kumak, Caac, Yuaga, Jawe, Pwâpwâ, Némi, Pwaamei, Fwâi, Pijé, Cémuhi and Paîci. Some dialects are also spoken in the Voh-Koné region. The most widely spoken language in this group is Paîci, with about 5000 speakers. Languages of this group are tonal, using different pitches to convey meaning.

Southern Languages

The 11 Kanak languages spoken in the south, from north to south, include Arhô, Arhâ, Ajië, Abwéwé, Néku, Nërë, Tîrî, Xârâcùù, Xârâgùrè, Dubéa and Kuniè. Ajië, the language of the Houaïlou region, is spoken on both coasts – it is one of the most widely spoken languages on Grande Terre today. The translation of a number of religious texts into Ajië, and a school at Houaïlou where Ajië is spoken, has given the language a certain prestige, to the detriment of neighbouring languages such as Paîci, which used to have about as many speakers. Ajië is also one of the few Kanak languages for which old written documents exist, including a diary published at the beginning of this century.

Languages of the Loyalty Islands

The Loyalty Islands (Iles Loyauté) group is made up of four languages, including the Polynesian language Faga Uvea, which is spoken on Uvéa, Nengône, spoken on Maré and Laai, spoken on Uvéa.

The fourth is Drehu, which is spoken on Lifou ('Lifou' is a European adaptation of the word Drehu, and the island Lifou may also be referred to as Drehu.) Nowadays, there are around 10,000 Drehu speakers, which makes it the most widely spoken Kanak language. The island's inhabitants are known as Atre Drehu, meaning 'the people of Drehu', and their language is called Qene Drehu, 'the Drehu language'. Unless specified, words and phrases in this chapter are from the Drehu language.

History

Due to the absence of written records, some forms in Kanak languages are able to be reconstructed only by comparing languages and cultures. The main factor in the near-disappearance of the languages in the 19th century was a sudden drop in population following the arrival of Europeans.

In 1863, a decree was issued banning the use of Kanak languages in schools, where French only was to be used. Today the situation is changing very slowly: there are five languages (Drehu, Nengône, Ajië, Paîci and Xârâcùù) which are offered at School-leaver's Certificate level, but there are not many places where they are taught.

No discussion of the languages of New Caledonia is complete without mentioning Pastor Maurice Leenhardt. Kanaks trained at his Do Néva mission were first taught to write, and then given the task of collecting as much material on Kanak languages as they could. This labour finally produced the *Langues et Dialectes de l'Austro-Mélanésie*, published in 1946, shortly before his death.

PRONUNCIATION
Vowels
Vowel sounds can be very different from English. A few of the more unusual are:

â	as the 'o' in 'on'
ë	as the 'an' in 'land'
ö	as the 'ou' in 'about'
ô	as the 'o' in 'long'
u	as the 'oo' in 'too'
û	like the 'oo' in 'too', but shorter

Consonants

c	as the 'ch' in 'cheque'
dr	as the 'd' in 'day'
g	as the 'ng' in 'camping'
j	as the 'j' in 'June'
hw	like a normal 'w' but with a puff of breath after it
ny	as the 'ny' in canyon
x	a guttural sound like the 'ch' in the Scottish 'loch'

MEETING PEOPLE
Greetings & Goodbyes

Greetings should be used with a great deal of care, as their meaning holds more importance than in some other places. In societies with an oral tradition, the spoken word is loaded with a power that it doesn't have in societies that use writing. It's not the done thing to address people in any old way. Greetings are considered an invitation to give details relating to identity, clan and origins, not just a polite formality as in the West.

Good day.	Bozu. (from French *bonjour*)
Greetings.	Talofa. (imported by Samoan teachers)
How are you?	Hapeu laï? (only asked by an adult – it's not polite to ask this of someone older than the speaker or of a stranger)
(reply)	Pëkö. (this reply is a gesture of politeness towards the adult who's asked the question)
Fine.	Kaloi.
Fine.	Egöcatr.
Who are you?	Drei nyipë (invitation to give details of one's identity)
I'm …	Ame ni tre …
I come from …	Ame la nojeng tre … (a declaration of one's origin and descent)

RICH & SUBTLE

Kanak languages don't distinguish between verbs and nouns, and there is no conjugation of words. However, the absence of distinct categories of nouns and verbs doesn't mean that they are 'simplified' languages. On the contrary, they have many subtle nuances and a rich variety of terms for directions, ways of facing and so on.

KANAK

Farewell. (on leaving the country)	Iahni.
See you tomorrow.	Elanyi hë.
Do you speak Lifou (Drehu)?	Hapeu atre hi nyipë la qene drehu?
Yes, I can speak a little Drehu.	Öö, eni a nango qene drehu.
Do you speak Engish?	Hapeu nyipë a qene papaale?
Do you speak French?	Hapeu nyipë a qene wiiwi?

Family & People

The vocabulary of kinship terms is very rich and complex, thus only a few terms are included here. Kinship terms vary according to the social position of the speaker, such as whether a person is senior, young, a father and so on. Terms are given in Drehu, Ajië and Nengone.

child	nëkö
children (in relation to their parents)	kuku
daughter (in relation to her parents)	kuku föe
father	kem
man	atr
mother	thin
senior; older sibling	nëkö haetra
son (in relation to his parents)	kuku trahmanyi
woman	föe

Etiquette

If you happen to be invited into someone's home, it's important to observe custom and ritual on arrival. This can vary according to the importance of your visit. Entrance doorways are made very low so that visitors are obliged to bend down as they come in. In the case of a simple visit, a little speech of thanks is enough. For a longer visit or a stay in the person's home, the ritual needs to be much more extensive, and includes, for instance, giving a manu (piece of cloth worn around the waist), money and/or food. The traditional phrase is Ame la qëameke i hun (here is our present), qëameke being the gift one makes on entering someone's home.

Here is my gift.	Ame la qëamekeng.
Here is our gift.	Ame la qëameke i hun.

KANAK

FOOD
Traditional Cooking

A traditional Kanak dish is the bougna, prepared by the 'food parcel' technique. The ingredients (root vegetables, bananas and coconut milk) are wrapped in banana leaves, then placed in a traditional pit oven dug in the ground, where they are cooked for a number of hours. Bougna may also be accompanied by chicken or fish.

On Lifou, bougna was once traditionally reserved for men, while children, women and the elderly had their own dishes. All stages, from preparing the oven to serving, are assigned according to the customary functions of family members.

banana	wahnawa
bread	falawa
coconut	ono
chicken/poultry	gutu
fish	i
freshwater fish	i ne hnetim
octopus	utr
sea fish	i ne hnagejë
shellfish	pelhë
taro	inagaj
water	tim
yam	koko

KANAKY

Although Kanaks, or Ti-Va-Ouere (Brothers of the Earth), are Melanesians (the group who inhabit many of the islands in the south-western Pacific), the country's indigenous people prefer to be called Kanaks, and many call their country Kanaky.

KANAK

GETTING AROUND

Kanak languages are remarkably rich in terms related to direction. They vary depending on where you are and where you're headed, and are also connected with clan histories and the establishment of the island's first inhabitants. People in New Caledonia are extremely interested in where you come from and where you're going. It's usually best to answer with your country of origin.

Where are you going? (what direction are you going in?)	Nyipë a tro ië?
Where are you going to? (what place are you headed for?)	Nyipë a tro ka?
I'm going …	Eni a tro e …
Where have you come from?	Qa i nyipë ka?
I'm coming from …	Qa …

towards	kowe
up/inland (towards the interior)	koho
down (towards the coast)	kuhu
over there (general term)	koilo

in a northerly direction	keepi
in a southerly direction	keejë
in an easterly direction	kehië
in a westerly direction	kehuë

Places & Habitats

cliffs	hugit
coast	kejë
crop planting zone	hnahlapa
forest	hnaxulu
inhabited zone	hnalapa
the interior	helepu
island	hnapeti

house	uma
sea	hnagejë
temple; sacred house	uma hmitrötre
traditional house; hut	uma meitro

Weather

What's the weather like today?	Tune ka la drai enehila?
It's sunny.	Kola jö.
It's raining.	Kola mani.
It's raining cats and dogs.	Kolo trotro la mani.
The rain has stopped.	Tha' kolo kö a mani.

fog/mist	xaxapo
rainbow	lewene
sky	hnengödrai

FESTIVALS

Avocado Festival
   held in mid to late May in Nece, Maré, to celebrate the end of the harvest, this is the island's largest fair

Bastille Day
   a military parade is held in the morning in central Noumea to commemorate the storming of the Bastille in 1789. The preceding evening there are fireworks, and people carrying lighted lanterns gather at dusk to form a procession that winds through the streets to Place des Cocotiers. Sometimes dance floors are set up here and bands entertain until late.

Équinoxe
   a diverse festival covering theatre, dance and music which is staged in Noumea every two years (odd numbered) in October

Festival of the Yam
   the most important Kanak festival, marking the beginning of the harvest, the Festival of the Yam is generally held around mid-March, around six months after the yams are planted. Having grown in the ancestral soil, the yam is

KANAK

considered sacred and thought to hold men's virility, thus ensuring that clans continue their lineage. They also determine the Kanak social calendar, and cultivation and harvesting of yams are filled with ritual designed to give thanks to the spirits. Many Kanaks living in Noumea return to their villages for this event.

The elders traditionally watch nature for signs indicating that the yam is ready. These include the appearance of certain stars, such as the Southern Cross, the call of a buzzard or the flowering of a particular tree. The official start of the harvest comes when the first yams are pulled from a sacred field and presented to the older clansmen and the chief. The roots are carried in a procession to the grande case, from where they are distributed among the tribe. Out of respect, the yam is never cut, but broken like bread.

Pacific Tempo
annual three-day event held in Noumea in mid to late May that showcases musicians from around the Pacific

Foire de Bourail
huge three-day agricultural fair held in Bourail in late August or early September. Features a rodeo, cattle show and sales, horseracing and a beauty pageant.

La Régate des Touques
contestants paddle furiously in decorative floats made from empty oil barrels in a race along Anse Vata. Takes place in Noumea in mid to late May.

Sound & Light Show
spectacular light shows are staged in late October/early November at Fort Teremba, near La Foa

KANAK

TIME & DATES
Days

The concept of naming the days of the week was introduced into the Drehu language by missionaries. However, the English names weren't adopted, and instead names were chosen that had relevance in post-missionary Drehu life. However, their use is becoming less frequent.

Monday	Thupene hmi (lit: after the holy day)
Tuesday	Drai ange dic (lit: day devoted to training teachers)
Wednesday	Drai menu (lit: ordinary day – without any religious education)
Thursday	Drai kaco (lit: day devoted to the religious education of the young)
Friday	Drai katru (lit: day devoted to the religious education of adults)
Saturday	Drai meci xen (lit: day for fasting in preparation for the Sabbath)
Sunday	Drai hmitrötr (lit: holy/sacred day)

DREHU PRONOUNS

I	eni/ni
you (sg)	nyipë/nyipö (f)
he	angeic/xapo (when the person isn't present)
it	ej
we (incl)	eashë/easo (when there are two), nyiso
we (excl)	eahun(i)
you	epun(i)
they (animate objects)	angaatr(e)
they (inanimate objects)	i tre ej

KANAK

Time

Drehu uses specific terms to express time and duration, as there are no tenses to express past, present and future.

four days ago	edrehnyij(e)
three days ago	edrexölepetr(e)
day before yesterday	edrehnë
yesterday	edrei
just now (in the past)	ekula
today	enehila
just now (in the future)	edrae hë
tomorrow	elanyi
day after tomorrow	euji
in three days' time	ecikön(e)
in four days' time	ecieke
once	ekö
in the future	hne drai epin
week	hmi
this week	e hmi celë
next week	e hmi ka troa xulu
last week	e hmi ka ase hë
this month	e treu celë
next month	e treu ka trao xulu
last month	e treu ka ase hë
month	treu (means 'the moon' also)

DREHU REDUPLICATION

A feature of Kanak languages is the reduplication of all or part of certain words to intensify their meaning in some way.

u	to cry; show oneself
uu	to communicate at a distance

Traditionally, the day is divided into several parts.

dawn	e hmakany(i) sine jidr(i)
morning	e hmakany(i)
middle of the day	e hmakany(i) hnaipajö
dusk	e hejihej(i)
night	e jidr(i)

KANAK LITERATURE

Coming from an oral tradition, Kanaks traditionally were masters of speech, with knowledge traditionally being passed on orally through poems, legends and stories. The written word was nonexistent in Kanak society until missionaries translated the Bible and a few other religious works into a couple of the Kanak languages. Although writing has never been a recognised art form, there are now a few contemporary Kanak authors.

La Présence Kanak by Jean-Marie Tjibaou gives an insight into the Kanak struggle for recognition and independence.

Tu Galala: Social Change in the Pacific is a collection of essays by indigenous writers from various Pacific nations. It describes the impact that growing poverty, nuclear testing, independence struggles, militarisation and social dislocation are having on Pacific Islanders. Susanna Ounei-Small, a Kanak author from Ouvéa, writes about the Matignon Accords or, as she describes it, 'the peace signed with our blood'.

Hwanfalik – Sayings from the Hienghène Valley by Kaloombat Tein offers an insight into the legends of the people of Hienghène and gives expressions in the Hienghène dialect, with explanations in English.

KANAK

NUMBERS

Drehu's numerical system is based on units of five (as with the digits of the hand), which makes for quite a complex counting system.

Cardinal Numbers

1	caas
2	luetr(e)
3	könitr(e)
4	eketr(e)
5	tripi
6	ca ngömen(e)
7	lue ngömen(e)
8	kôni ngömen(e)
9	eke ngömen(e)
10	lue pi ngömen(e)
11	ca ko
12	lua ko
13	kôni ko
14	eke ko
15	kon pi
16	caa gai hnao
17	lue gai hnao
18	kâni gai hnao
19	eke gai hnao
20	caa atr
21	catr(e) nge caas
22	catr(e) nge luetre
23	catr(e) nge könitr(e)
24	catr(e) nge eketre
25	catr(e) nge tripi
26	catr(e) nge ca ngöme
27	catr(e) nge lue ngöm
28	catr(e) tige köni ngö
29	catr(e) nge eke ngöm
30	catr(e) nge luepi
40	lue atr(e)

THE AJIË LANGUAGE
People & Family

children (in relation to their parents)	pâle
daughter (in relation to her parents)	peva
junior; younger sibling	padi
man	wi
mother	pani
senior; older sibling	pavariè
son (in relation to his parents)	xie
woman	boé

Food

banana	kwijèi
coconut	nu (pwê nu fruit)
chicken/poultry	manu
crab	nya

AJIË PRONOUNS

The Ajië language uses dual pronouns, which are used for two people, as well as plural forms, which indicate more than two.

singular	I	gènya
	you (sg)	gèi
	he/she/it	ce
dual	we two (incl)	görru
	two of us (excl)	gövu
	you two	göu
	those two	curu
plural	we (incl)	gèvé
	you (excl)	gèrré
	you	gëvë
	they	céré

KANAK

fish	éwâ
flying fox	méu
octopus	yaaru
shellfish	êê maa
taro	mwa
yam	mëu

Oral History

Oral history has a major political and cultural role in New Caledonia. It is the means by which clan histories and origins are recorded, as well as the ownership of property. This in fact makes the subject a particularly sensitive one, since often each clan has a different version of the same story.

Kanak oral history takes different forms, depending on the age of the audience and the purpose of storytelling. Children's oral history is recited by parents or grandparents, and is accompanied by a whole set of gestures such as tickling and onomatopoeic noises to hold the young listeners' attention. Children also tell stories to one another.

Children's tales can be told on various levels. The most simple can be understood by very young children, and their purpose is to amuse and to develop memory and listening skills. The stories are usually anthropomorphic about animals, which entertains the audience and gets them used to the flora and fauna of their natural environment.

Other levels of these stories are revealed to children as they get older. These recitals contain all the fundamental rules of society and of community living. Because they become familiar with these stories from their earliest years, children also pick up the social codes of their group, such as sexual norms and marriage taboos.

The following story is from the Ajië language, spoken in the Houaïlou region.

KANAK

Vi nimö né méu (The Tale of the Flying Fox)

Na taa mâ na méu,
>   There was once a flying fox,

na bôri kâi bââwê.
>   who ate figs.

Na bôri kâi rôi pwêê-è,
>   She ate all the fruit from the fig tree,

na böri kwârßà dee-é,
>   she ate all the leaves,

na böri kî yè barße kwèè-è,
>   she ate the roots,

na böri kwârßâ barße.
>   and chewed them.

Na böri pwa mi na dèxâ népuruu kwa,
>   It started to rain,

na böri êrße, 'üüüü ... na dö kwaiö
>   and she cried, 'ooohh ... it's raining on the

nékaré arii i pâ örßökau!
>   sacred basket of the chiefs!

Gö yè mâ dö vi xara rö-wè rö-a?'
>   Now where can take it?'

Na böri cêê vi, na mâ cêê vi, na mâ cêê vi ...
>   She flew and flew and flew ...

na mâ cêê pwa rö dèxâ mwâérße.
>   until she came to a cave.

Na böri vi ru rö-i,
>   She went in,

na böri tö-i.
>   and there she stayed.

Na böri cuu mi na dèxâ èmènürßü mâ kuxè-è,
>   A black ant crept up and bit her,

na böri êrße, 'kixâ, kixâ, kixâ ...'
>   and she cried, 'Oh, oh, oh ...'

The first part of this tale describes the natural environment (the flying fox, the fig-tree), as well as teaching vocabulary, with terms for different eating actions (eating meat, eating fibre, eating condiments).

KANAK

The flying fox is very mobile, and represents the changes of the individual's position within the social group – it is an element of instability. The fig-tree is the image of the group, immobile and stable. It represents the connection of the group with the land, and with its past and origins.

The boundless appetite of the flying fox (she eats every bit of the fig-tree) refers to deviant sexual behaviour, such as not respecting the rules of marriage, or the incest taboo. Her eating fruit, leaves and roots can be interpreted as her having sexual relations with all the age classes of the group.

The infringement of the marriage rules is made worse by the presence of the sacred basket, which is used to carry the treasures of the group in matrimonial exchanges. The rain falling on it is an external element, which upsets the stability of this universe a little more – a clear indication that the clan is in danger.

At the story's end, the flying fox finds herself in an unknown place, which is therefore a place of danger. This is a cave – one of the places for burying the dead – which reinforces the idea of her social death and casting-out. When the ant bites the flying fox, this confirms her status as an outcast.

THE NENGONE LANGUAGE
People & Family

boy	haicahman
child	tenen
father; maternal uncle	cecen
girl	haerow
grandchild/grandparent	wabuaien
grandfather/grandmother (maternal)	pa
grand tribal chief	doku
man	cahman/cahan
mother; maternal aunt	hma ni; hma nien
people/population	nod
member of a tribe	celuaien
woman	hmenew
uncle (maternal)	hmi/hmihmi

KANAK

Numbers

As with Drehu, Nengone's numerical system is based on units of five.

Cardinal Numbers

0	dekosa
1	sa
2	rewe
3	tini
4	ece
5	sedong (se)
6	sedong ne sa (sedosa)
7	sedorew
8	sedotin
9	sedoec
10	ruenin (rue)
11	rueninesa (ruesa)
12	ruerewo
13	ruetinko
14	rueeco
15	adenin (ade)i
16	adeninesa (adesa)ai hnao
17	aderewi hnao
18	adetingai hnao
19	adeecai hnao
20	sarengom (sare)r
21	sarengom ne sa (saresa) nge caas
22	sarerew nge luetre
23	saretin
24	sareec
25	saresedong
26	saresedosan(e)
27	saresedorewen(e)
28	saresedotinmen(e)
29	saresedoecen(e)
30	saregom ne ruenin
40	ruengom

100	sedong re ngom (sedongom)
200	rue sedongom
300	ade sedongom
400	ece sedongom
500	sedosedongom

Ordinal numbers

1st	hnapan(e)
2nd	hnaluen(e)
3rd	hnakônin(e)
4th	hnaeken
5th	hnatripin(e)

MAORI

NEW ZEALAND

TASMAN SEA

North Cape

SOUTH PACIFIC OCEAN

Kaitaia

Whangarei

Dargaville

Great Barrier Island

Cape Colville

Auckland

Thames

East Cape

Huntly

Hamilton

Tauranga

Bay of Plenty

Rotorua

Gisborne

Lake Taupo

Taupo

New Plymouth

Napier

Cape Egmont

Hastings

Wanganui

Palmerston North

Cape Farewell

Masterton

Nelson

WELLINGTON

Richmond

Blenheim

Cook Strait

Westport

Greymouth

Kaikoura

Hokitika

Mt Cook (3755)

Christchurch

Banks Peninsula

Ashburton

TASMAN SEA

Canterbury Bight

Lake Wanaka

Timaru

Wanaka

Queenstown

Oamaru

Lake Te Anau

Lake Wakatipu

Te Anau

Dunedin

SOUTH PACIFIC OCEAN

West Cape

Invercargill

Foveaux Strait

Oban

Stewart Island (Rakiura)

0   100   200 km

Inset map

International Date Line

Equator

Australia

South Pacific Ocean

New Zealand

MAORI

INTRODUCTION

New Zealand has two official languages – English and Maori (written as Māori in the Maori language). Although English is spoken throughout New Zealand, around 500,000 New Zealander's also speak Maori, although only around six percent have a high degree of fluency.

Although the Maori language was once on the decline, it has now made a strong comeback. Although English is widely spoken, there are some occasions when knowing a little Maori would be useful – such as when visiting a marae (ancestral meeting place), where often only Maori is spoken.

Although the Maori language never died out – it's always been used in Maori ceremonial events – with the renaissance of Maoritanga, or Maori culture, there's been a revival of interest in the language, which is an important part of . Many Maori people who'd heard the language at marae all their lives, but hadn't spoken it on a day-to-day basis, are now studying Maori and are speaking it with some fluency. Maori is also taught in schools throughout New Zealand. Some TV programs and news reports are broadcast in Maori, many placenames are being renamed in Maori.

Many young children are taught Maori language and culture, so they will grow up speaking Maori in addition to English, and be familiar with Maori tradition. On some marae, only Maori is allowed to be spoken, which encourages its use and emphasises the distinct Maori character of the marae.

History

Maori are the original Polynesian settlers of New Zealand. They migrated from the islands of the South Pacific around 800 AD, and the Maori language and culture is closely related to those of other Polynesian peoples, including Hawaiian, Tahitian and Rarotongan Maori. The Maori have a vividly chronicled history, recorded in songs and chants which dramatically recall the Great

MAORI

Migration and other important events. It was the early European missionaries who first recorded the language in written form, using only 15 letters of the English alphabet, with all syllables ending in a vowel.

PRONUNCIATION

Maori is a fluid, poetic language which is surprisingly easy to pronounce if you just remember to say it phonetically and split each word (some can be amazingly long) into separate syllables.

Vowels

Each vowel is pronounced with either a long or a short sound. When learning to speak Maori, the correct pronunciation of the vowels is all important. The sounds are only approximated here – to really get it right, you'll have to hear someone pronounce it correctly.

Short Vowels

a	as the 'u' in 'but'
e	as the 'e' in 'egg'
i	as the 'i' in 'it'
o	like the 'o' in 'more'
u	as the 'oo' in 'foot'

Long Vowels

ā	as the 'a' in 'large'
ē	a sound that falls between the 'e' in 'get' and the 'ai' in 'bait'
ī	as the 'ee' in 'weed'
ō	as the 'o' in 'pork'
ū	as the 'oo' in 'moon'

Diphthongs

ae	as the 'i' in 'dire'
ai	as the 'y' in 'my'
ao/au	as the 'ow' in 'how'
ea	as the 'ai' in 'lair'

ei	as the 'ay' in 'bay'
eo	pronounced *eh-oh*
eu	pronounced *eh-oo*
ia	as the 'ee' in 'beer'
ie	as the 'ye' in 'yet'
io	as the 'ye o' in 'ye old'
iu	as the 'ue' in 'cue'
oa	as the 'oa' in 'roar'
oe	as the 'awe' in 'raw eggs'
oi	as the 'oy' in 'toy'
ou	as the 'ew' in 'sew'
ua	as the 'ewe' in 'fewer'

Each syllable ends in a vowel. There's never more than one vowel in a syllable, and there are no silent letters.

Consonants

Most consonants in Maori – h, k, m, n, p, t and w – are pronounced much the same as in English. The Maori r is a flapped sound with the tongue near the front of the mouth, and is like English 'l'. The pronunciation of t depends on the vowel which follows it. When followed by 'i' or 'u', the tongue touches the roof of the mouth. When followed by 'e', 'o' or 'u', the tongue touches just behind the teeth.

Two combinations of consonants require special attention. The letters ng, pronounced as in the English suffix '-ing', can be used at the beginning of words as well as at the end. It's easy to practise this sound, just say 'ing' over and over, isolate the ng part of it, and then practise using it to begin a word rather than end one.

The wh also has a unique pronunciation in Maori, generally being pronounced like a soft English 'f'. This pronunciation is used in many placenames in New Zealand, especially in the North Island, which has placenames such as Whangarei, Whangaroa and Whakapapa (all pronounced as if they began with a soft 'f'). There is some regional variation, however. In the region around the Whanganui River, for example, the wh is pronounced the same as in English (as in 'when').

MEETING PEOPLE
Greetings & Goodbyes

Maori greetings are becoming increasingly popular – don't be surprised if you're greeted on the phone or on the street with Kia ora.

Haere mai.	Welcome.
Kia ora.	Hello; Good luck; Good health.
Tēnā koe.	Hello. (to one person)
Tēnā kōrua.	Hello. (to two people)
Tēnā koutou.	Hello. (to three or more people)
Kei te pehea koe?	How are you? (to one person)
Kei te pehea korua?	How are you? (to two people)
Kei te pehea koutou?	How are you? (to three or more people)
Kei te pai.	Very well, thank you.
Haere rā.	Goodbye. (from someone staying behind to someone leaving)
E noho rā.	Goodbye. (from someone leaving to someone staying behind)
hongi	Maori greeting involving the pressing of noses and the sharing of life breath
pōwhiri	a traditional welcome onto the marae (see page 100)

People

atua	spirit or gods
hoa	friend
kaumātua	elders; highly respected members of a tribe; the people you would ask for permission to enter a marae
Māui	important figure in Maori mythology

Mōriori	inhabitants of the Chatham Islands
ngāti	people/tribe (called ngai in the South Island)
Pākehā	white or European person
tāne	man
tangata	the people; human beings
tangata whenua	people of the land; local people
taniwha	fear-inspiring water spirit
tohunga	priest; wizard; general expert
wahine	woman
wairua	spirit

MAORI

Family

Maori society is tribal, and many Maori refer to themselves in terms of their iwi (tribe), as with the name Ngati Kahu (descendent of Kahu). In traditional times, tribes were headed by an ariki (supreme chief), but the hapu (subtribe) was often more relevant in everyday life, and village structure was based around whanau (extended family groups). The whanau remains an important part of modern Maori culture.

MAORI WARRIORS

Traditionally, one of the best ways to promote the mana (spiritual power or prestige) of a tribe was through battle, so the Maori had a highly developed warrior society. War had its own worship, sacrifices, rituals, dances and art forms. Tribes battled over territory or for utu (revenge), with the losers often being enslaved or eaten. Eating an enemy was the ultimate insult, and was thought to pass on the enemy's life force (mauri) or power. The Maori built pa (defensive villages) where they retreated when under attack.

MAORI

Whakapapa (genealogies) determines people's place in a tribe, as ancestral and family ties are critical. The marae (sacred area of an ancestral meeting place) is the focus of Maori culture.

aunt	whaea; matua kēkē; āti; whaene
brother (girl speaking)	tungāne
brother (younger boy speaking)	tuakana
brother (older boy speaking)	teina
brother-in-law (of female)	autāne
brother-in-law (of male)	taokete
father	matua tāne; pāpā
father-in-law	hungawai/hunarei
mother	whaea; matua wahine; māmā
mother-in-law	hungawai/hungarei
sister (of female)	tuakana (older)
	teina (younger)
sister (of male)	tuahine
sister-in-law (of female)	taokete
sister-in-law (of male)	auwahine
uncle	matua kēkē

Marae Etiquette

Perhaps the best place to gain some understanding of Maoritanga (Maori culture) is by visiting a marae. The marae ātea is the open area in front of the meeting house, or wharenui, but the term is often loosely used to describe the buildings as well. The marae is sacred to the Maori, and should be treated with great respect. Some of the aspects of Maori culture like the pōwhiri, the formal welcome, are now an accepted part of New Zealand culture.

Some of the customs and conventions of the marae include:

karanga
　the plaintive wail given by the kuia (elder women) to welcome and farewell visitors and the dead

MAORI

kaumatua
     the term given to the elderly, who have a favoured status in
     Maori society. They provide leadership, wise counsel and
     knowledge of protocol and tribal history.

manaakitanga
     the act of caring for visitors and promoting friendship, or
     wairua. The marae is a place of tremendous pride, history
     and spirituality, and is connected to past events.

mauri
     the intangible life force that's the essence of the marae.
     Mauri is cared for and kept alive by the home people, and is
     never allowed to leave or to be taken by visitors. When
     speaking, a person is said to have the mauri of the marae.

tangata whenua
     a formal funeral that's usually held on a marae. Lasting three
     days, tangata whenua give an opportunity for people to pay
     their last respects, and are occasions where traditional customs
     are enacted.

tangi
     the home of people whose job it is to make their visitors
     comfortable and well fed

tūrangawaewae
     the term given to a person's home or (adopted) marae. It is
     where that person can speak with authority.

TE REO MAORI

The Māori language is under threat, as most native
speakers are over 50 years old. The Kōhanga Reo
(language nests for young children) and Kura Kaupapa
(primary schools) have increased the number of speakers,
although the language spoken is often modelled on
English grammatical structures.

waiata

> a wonderful custom that requires each speech made on the Maori to be followed by a song

whaikōrero

> speech making. Maori oratory on the marae is highly ritualised.

whanaungatanga

> togetherness. The dynamics of the marae allow visitors to whakapapa, or 'connect genealogy' with the home of the people, so they can become tangata whenua, 'people of the land'

A welcoming ritual, te pōwhiri ki te manuhiri, is followed every time visitors (manuhiri) come onto the marae. They bring with them the memories of their dead. The hosts (tangata whenua) pay their respects to the deceased of the manuhiri, likewise the manuhiri to the tangata whenua. The ceremony removes the tapu (taboo) and permits the manuhiri and tangata whenua to interact. The practice varies from marae to marae. Note that shoes must be removed before entering a whare hui.

Te powhiri ki te manuhiri may often begin with the welcoming call (karanga) by women of the tangata whenua to the manuhiri. It could also include a ceremonial challenge (taki/wero). The manuhiri reply to the karanga and proceed on to the marae. They pay their respects and sit where indicated, generally to the left (if facing outwards) of the whare hui.

Welcoming speeches (mihi) are given by the tangata whenua from the threshold (Taumata Tapu) in front of the meeting house. Each speech is generally supported by a song (waiata), generally led by the women. When the mihi is finished the manuhiri reply. The tapu is deemed to have been lifted from the manuhiri when the replies are finished. The manuhiri then greet the tangata whenua with handshakes and the pressing of noses (hongi). In some places the hongi is a single press, in others it is press, release, press.

Before the manuhiri leave the marae they make farewell speeches (poroporoaki) which take the form of thanks and prayer.

The important thing to remember, as a visitor, is that once invited, you're extremely welcome on the marae, as a cornerstone of Maori culture is hospitality. Once protocol has been satisfied, you have become part of an extended family and the concern of the tangata whenua is you – the manuhiri. They want to see you fed and looked after, almost spoiled, because you're a guest. Such hospitality is fantastic and lucky visitors to New Zealand are increasingly being given the opportunity to enjoy it, either as a guest or on one of the marae tours that are becoming popular. If you do receive hospitality such as food and lodging, it is customary to offer a koha or donation to help towards the upkeep of the marae. When the roles are reversed and you are the tangata whenua, remember that the care of *your* guests becomes your first concern.

MAORI

MAORI LITERATURE

Witi Ihimaera is a prolific Maori author of novels and short stories, including *The Matriarch, Tangi* and *Pounamu, Pounamu*. His novel *Bulibasha* looks at Maori sheep-shearing gangs of the North Island.

Keri Hulme won the British Booker McConnell Prize for fiction with *The Bone People* in 1985, and has published several other novels and books of poetry.

Alan Duff writes about Maori people in modern New Zealand. His novels (*Once Were Warriors* and *One Night Out Stealing*) and non-fiction work *Maori: The Crisis and the Challenge* have generated heated debate.

Other significant Maori authors include novelists Apirana Taylor, Patricia Grace and poet Hone Tuwhare.

Te Whakahuatanga o te Ao – Reflections of Reality provides an anthology of written and oral Maori literature, while an examination of issues affecting Maori people by prominent Maori authors can be found in *He Whakaatanga o te Ao – The Reality*.

MAORI

FOOD

The provision of food is the manifestation of the Maori peoples' heightened sense of hospitality. A lot of energy goes into the preparation of food for visitors. Tribes living on the coast provide seafood for their relatives inland and, likewise, inland tribes provide delicacies not available on the coast, like eels and kereru (pigeon).

abalone	pāua
corn (fermented)	kānga pirau
crayfish	koura
earth oven	hāngi
feast	hākari
huhu bugs, dug from rotting trees	huhu
mussels	kuku/kūtai
mutton bird	titī
sea urchins (a Maori delicacy)	kina
shellfish	kaimoana
shellfish (large)	toheroa
shellfish (small)	tuatua
sweet potato	kūmara
wild sow thistle	pūhā
young fern shoots	pikopiko

GETTING AROUND
Placenames

Many New Zealand placenames are made up of Maori words.

anatoki	axe or adze in a cave; cave or valley in the shape of an axe
awa	river or valley
ika	fish
iti	small
kahurangi	treasured possession; special greenstone

kai	food
kainga	village (unfortified)
kare	rippling
kotinga	boundary line
koura	crayfish
manga	branch/stream/tributary
mangarakau	plenty of sticks; a great many trees
manu	bird
maunga	mountain
moana	sea/lake
moko	tattoo
motu	island
nui	big
o	of
one	beach/sand/mud
onekaka	red-hot sand
pa	fortified village (usually on a hilltop)
papa	flat, broad slab
parapara	soft mud used for dyeing flax
patarua	killed by the thousands (site of early tribal massacres)
pohatu	stone
puke	hill
rangi	sky/heavens
rangiheata	absence of clouds; a range seen in the early morning

MAORI

DID YOU KNOW ... The higher social classes adorned themselves with intricate tattoos. Women had moko (facial tattoos) on their chins while high-ranking men tattooed their entire face, as well as their buttocks and other parts of the body.

MAORI

repo	swamp
roa	long
roto	lake
rua	hole,/two
takaka	killing stick for parrot; bracken
tane	man
tata	close to; dash against; twin islands
te	the
totaranui	place of big totara trees
uruwhenua	enchanted objects
wahine	woman
wai	water
waikaremumu	bubbling waters
waingaro	lost; waters that disappear in certain seasons
wainui	big bay; many rivers; the ocean
waka	canoe
wero	challenge
whanau	extended family
whanga	bay or inlet
whare	house
whenua	land/country

Try a few – Whanga-roa is 'long bay', Roto-rua is 'two lakes', Roto-roa is 'long lake', Wai-kare-iti is 'little rippling water'. All those names containing wai – Waitomo, Waitara, Waioru, Wairoa, Waitoa, Waihi and so on – are associated with water.

Aoraki	Mt Cook (lit: the cloud piercer)
Aotearoa	New Zealand (lit: land of the long white cloud. Also referred to as the 'land of the wrong white crowd')
Te Ika a Maui	the North Island (lit: fish of Maui, a demigod)
pakihi	(pronounced *par-kee*) unproductive land on South Island's west coast

Rakiura	(lit: land of glowing skies) Stewart Island, which is important in Maori mythology as Te punga a Maui, the anchor of Maui's canoe
Tāmaki-makau-rau	Auckland (lit: land of a hundred lovers)
Te Wai Pounamu	the South Island, known in mythology as Te waka a Maui, Maui's canoe
Te matau a Maui	Mahia Peninsula, on the east coast of North Island (lit: Maui's fish-hook)

MAORI

Seasons

autumn	ngahuru
spring	kōanga
summer	raumati
winter	hōtoke/takurua/makariri

Souvenirs & Artefacts

hei tiki	small carving of a human figure which is worn around the neck, often representing an ancestor. Also called a tiki.
manaia	traditional carving design (lit: bird-headed man)

THE LONGEST PLACENAME IN THE WORLD

Take a deep breath and then spit this out as fast as you can (it helps to split it into its component parts).

Taumata-whaka-tangi-hanga-koa-uauo-tamatea-turipu-kakapiki-maunga-horo-nuku-pokai-whenua-kita-natahu

According to the *Guinness Book of Records*, it means 'The place where Tamatea, the man with the big knees, who slid, climbed, and swallowed mountains, known as land eater, played his flute to his loved one'.

MAORI

mere	flat, greenstone war club
nui	carved ceremonial poles of peace and war
tukutuku	wall panellings in marae and churches
waka	war canoe

LEGENDS
Creation of the Earth & Sky

In the beginning there was nothingness. Before the light, there was only darkness.

Rangi nui, the sky, dwelt with Papa tu a nuku, the Earth. The two were united and bore many children. Papa's nakedness was covered with many things begotten from her union with Rangi – land, trees, animals of the sea and many other created things – so that she would not be naked. But all lived in utter darkness.

Rangi (Sky-Father) and Papa (Earth-Mother) had six important children. They were Tawhiri matea, god of winds and storms; Tangaroa, god of the sea and of all things living in it; Tane mahuta, god of the forest and of all things that live in the forest; Haumia tiketike, god of wild plants that give food for humankind, including the fern root, berries and many others; Rongo ma Tane, god of cultivated food, including the kumara and all other plants cultivated for food by humankind; and Tu matauenga, the god of war.

After aeons and aeons of living in darkness, because their parents were joined together and no light had ever yet come between them, the children of Rangi and Papa could take it no longer – they wanted light. They debated what they should do. Eventually, they decided they should separate their parents so that light could enter the world.

They each tried, and failed, to separate Rangi and Papa. Finally, it was Tane mahuta's turn to try, and he pushed and strained, his shoulders to the ground and his feet to the sky, and finally succeeded in forcing his parents apart. Light flooded into the world. Thus Tane mahuta became father of the day.

The two parents were grief-stricken at having been separated.

They have been separated ever since, but their love for one another has never faded. In the beginning, Rangi shed so many tears that much of the land that had been revealed to light became covered by sea. Finally some of their children turned Papa over onto her stomach, so that Rangi and Papa would not always be looking at one another and grieving.

Rangi still cries for his wife, but not as much as before when there was a danger that all the land would be drowned because of his tears – his tears now are the drops of dew that form every night on Papa's back. The mists that form in the mornings in the valleys, and rise towards the heavens, are Papa's sighs of longing for her husband.

Creation of New Zealand

A long time after the creation of the world – after Tane mahuta, god of the forest, had created a woman out of red earth, breathed life into her nostrils, mated with her and had a daughter (who also became his wife and bore him other daughters) and after many other things had happened – the demigod Maui, who lived in Hawaiki, went out fishing with his brothers.

They went further and further out to sea. When they were a long way out, Maui took out his magic fish-hook (the jaw of his sorcerer grandmother), tied it to a strong rope, and then dropped it over the side of the canoe. Soon he caught an immense fish and, struggling mightily, pulled it up.

This fish became the North Island of New Zealand, called the ancient name of Maori Te ika a Maui (the fish of Maui) or sometimes Te ikaroa a Maui (the big fish of Maui). The Mahia Peninsula, at the north end of Hawke Bay on the east coast of the North Island, was known as Te matau a Maui (the fish-hook of Maui), since it was the hook with which he caught the giant fish.

The South Island was known as Te waka a Maui, or the canoe of Maui, in which he was sitting when he caught the fish. Kaikoura Peninsula, on the north-east coast of the South Island, was the seat of the canoe. Another name for the South Island was Te wai

Pounamu (the water greenstone), since much greenstone (jade, or pounamu) was found in the rivers there.

Stewart Island, south of the South Island, was known as Te punga a Maui (the anchor of Maui). It was the anchor that held the canoe as Maui hauled in the giant fish.

Hinemoa & Tutanekai

The story of Hinemoa and Tutanekai is one of the best-known lovers' tales in New Zealand. It is not a legend but a true story, though you may hear one or two variations. The descendants of Hinemoa and Tutanekai still live in the Rotorua area today.

THE HAKA

The haka is the Maori war chant that precedes a battle. Delivered with fierce shouting, flexing arm movements that resemble fists pummelling the side of someone's head, and thunderous stamping to grind whatever is left into the dust, it is indeed a frightening sight. Made famous by the All Blacks national rugby team, it can scare even the spectators in the stands, let alone the opponents on the field.

Each tribe has its own haka, but the most famous comes from Te Rauparaha (1768–1849), chief of the Ngati Toa tribe (see page 11). He was one of the last great warrior chiefs, carving a course of mayhem from Waikato to the South Island, where European settlers and many southern Maori were slaughtered by his advance.

It's said to have originated when Te Rauparaha was fleeing from his enemies. A local chief hid him in an underground kumara store, where Te Rauparaha waited in the dark, expecting to be found. When the store was opened and the sun shone in, it was not his enemies but the hairy local chief telling him they had gone. Te Rauparaha climbed the ladder to perform this victorious haka.

MAORI

TE RAUPARAHA'S HAKA

Ka mate, ka mate
　It is death, it is death
Ka ora, ka ora
　It is life, it is life
Ka mate, ka mate
　It is death, it is death
Ka ora, ka ora
　It is life, it is life
Tēnei te tangata pūhuruhuru
　This is the hairy man
Nānā i tiki mai whakawhiti te rā
　Who caused the sun to shine again for me
ūpāne, ūpāne
　Up the ladder, up the ladder
ūpāne kaupāne
　Up to the top
Whiti te rā
　The sun shines

Hinemoa was a young woman of a subtribe that lived on the western shore of Lake Rotorua. Tutanekai was a young man of the subtribe who lived on Mokoia Island, on the lake.

The two subtribes sometimes visited one another, and that was how Hinemoa and Tutanekai met. But though both were of high birth in their respective tribes, Tutanekai was illegitimate and so, while the family of Hinemoa thought he was a fine young man and could see that the two young people loved one another, they were not in favour of them marrying.

At night, Tutanekai would play his flute on the island, and sometimes the wind would carry his melody across the water to Hinemoa. In his music she could hear his declaration of love for her. Her people, meanwhile, took to tying up the canoes at night to make sure she could not take off and go to him.

MAORI

Finally, one night, as she heard Tutanekai's music wafting over the waters, Hinemoa was so overcome with longing that she could stand it no longer. She peeled off her clothes to get rid of the weight and set off to swim the long distance from the shore to the island. In some versions of the story she also buoyed herself up with calabash gourds.

When she arrived on Mokoia, Hinemoa was in a quandary. She had had to shed her clothing in order to swim to the island, but now there, she could scarcely walk into the settlement naked! She sought refuge in a hot pool and tried to figure out what to do next.

Time passed and eventually a man came to fetch water from a cold spring beside the hot pool. Disguising her voice as a man's, Hinemoa called out, 'Who is it?' The man replied that he was the slave of Tutanekai, come to fetch water. Hinemoa reached out of the darkness, seized the calabash and broke it. This happened a few more times, until finally Tutanekai himself came to the pool and demanded that the interloper identify himself. He was amazed when it turned out to be Hinemoa.

Tutanekai stole Hinemoa into his hut. In the morning, when Tutanekai was sleeping very late, a slave was sent to wake him and came back reporting that someone else was also sleeping in Tutanekai's bed! The two lovers emerged, and when Hinemoa's efforts to reach Tutanekai had been revealed, their union was celebrated.

TIME & DATES
Days

Monday	Mane; Rā tuatahi
Tuesday	Tūrei; Rā tuarua
Wednesday	Wenerei; Rā tuatoru
Thursday	Tāite; Rā tuawhā
Friday	Paraire; Rā tuarima
Saturday	Hātarei; Rā horoi
Sunday	Rā tapu

SONG: POKAREKARE ANA

Pokarekare ana is New Zealand's most cherished traditional song. It was adapted from a poem by Paraire Henare Tomoana (1868–1946) of the Ngati Kahungunu tribe. Although his original lyrics weren't about Rotorua, but rather Waiapu, the words seemed to fit the story of Hinemoa and Tutanekai so perfectly that in popular song the lake's name was changed to Rotorua.

Pōkarekare ana ngā wai o Rotorua.
  Troubled are the waters of Rotorua.
Whiti atu koe, e hine, marino ana ē.
  If you cross them, oh maiden, they will be calm.

Chorus
E hine ē, hoki mai rā,
  Come back to me, maiden,
Ka mate ahau i te aroha ē.
  I love you so much.

E kore te aroha e maroke i te rā.
  My love will never dry in the sun.
Mākūkū tonu i aku roimata ē.
  It will always be wet with my tears.

Repeat Chorus
Tuhi atu taku reta, tuku atu taku rīngi.
  I have written my letter, I have sent my ring.
Kei kite tō iwī, raruraru ana ē.
  If your people see them, there will be trouble.

Repeat Chorus
Kua whati taku pēne, kua pau aku pepa,
  My pen is broken, my paper is all used up.
Engari te aroha, mau tonu ana ē.
  But my love for you will always remain.

MAORI

Months

January	Hānuere
February	Pepuere
March	Māehe
April	āperira
May	Mei
June	Hune
July	Hūrae
August	ākuhata
September	Hepetema
October	Oketopa
November	Nōema
December	Tīhema

NUMBERS

1	tahi
2	rua
3	toru
4	whā
5	rima
6	ono
7	whitu
8	waru
9	iwa

FESTIVALS

The Aotearoa Traditional Maori Performing Arts Festival is held in Wellington in the February of odd-numbered years.

The Ngaruawahia Regatta for Maori Canoes is held in Hamilton every year in March.

10	tekau
11	tekau mā tahi
12	tekau mā rua
13	tekau mā toru
14	tekau mā whaa
15	tekau mā rima
16	tekau mā ono
17	tekau mā whitu
18	tekau mā waru
19	tekau mā iwa
20	rua tekau
21	tekau mā tahi
22	tekau mā rua
23	tekau mā toru

MAORI

MAORI

30	toru tekau
31	tekau mā rima
40	whā tekau
50	rima tekau
60	ono tekau
70	whitu tekau
80	waru takau
90	iwa tekau
100	rau
200	e rua rau
1000	mano
one million	miriona

NIUE

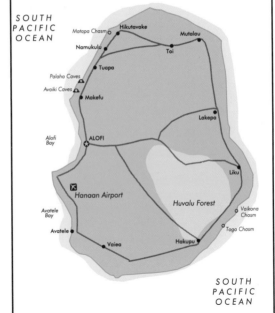

NIUE

0   3   6 km

SOUTH
PACIFIC
OCEAN

Matapa Chasm   Hikutavake
Namukulu   Mutalau
            Tuapa   Toi
Palaha Caves
Avaiki Caves
            Makefu
                            Lakepa
Alofi
Bay   ALOFI
                            Liku
            Hanaan Airport
                    Huvalu Forest
Avatele   Vaikona
Bay   Chasm
Avatele   Togo Chasm
        Vaiea   Hakupu

SOUTH
PACIFIC
OCEAN

NIUEAN

INTRODUCTION

Niue is located 2400km north-east of New Zealand, about 120km east of the International dateline, within a triangle made up of Tonga, Samoa and the Cook Islands. Niue has a population of approximately 2000 people, with an additional 14,000 Niueans living in New Zealand. With its tiny population, Niue is the smallest self-governing state in the world. It's democratically elected government has a Legislative Assembly of only 20 members. Niue has a free association with New Zealand citizens, and Niueans are issued with New Zealand passports.

It's easy to get around in Niue using only English, since nearly all Niueans are bilingual, except for the very young and the very old. Niue's only secondary school is based on the New Zealand school curriculum, and students begin studying English in their first year. Television, radio, public signs and official forms are in English, and people in the tourism industry speak English fluently.

Despite the prevalance of English, it's important to remember that English is spoken as a second language in Niue, so some confusion is possible if you engage in lengthy conversations. You'll notice that Niueans speak to each other in their own tongue. If you speak English, Niueans will expect you to speak English with them, and will address you in English. However, Niueans are usually thrilled when visitors attempt to speak their language. Don't be surprised if your first attempts at Niuean are met with laughing and giggling. This is likely to be an expression of surprise, as relatively few visitors try to speak Niuean. Niueans don't mean to offend, and will happily speak slowly and repeat themselves in an effort to help you understand. Your first attempts at Niuean are likely to be met with the comment Iloilo lahi a koe!, which means 'You're very smart!'.

History

Ancestors of the Niuean people came from Tonga and Samoa some 1500 years ago, and there are still many similiarities between the three languages. There has been plenty of discussion as to who came first, the Tongans or Samoans, but Niueans stick to their oral traditions, which agree that the land was first populated by five tupua (gods) from Fonuagalo (lost land or unknown land). Whether the original land was named Fonuagalo to deliberately hide their originating country, or whether they actually came from Lalofonua (land below or underworld) is not known, but in Niue it's generally thought that the gods had great powers and succeeded in building up the land.

PRONUNCIATION

Niuean pronunciation isn't especially difficult for the English speaker, since most of the sounds are similar to those found in English. The traditional Niuean alphabet uses only 17 letters. When speaking to a Niuean, however, be aware that many English words may be incorporated and 'Niueanised', which may include non-traditional pronunciation. Many younger Niueans are so comfortable with English vocabulary that they'll use their own versions of uncommon words rather than remember the Niuean word. For example, a teenaged Niuean may not know that tafuā means 'whale', but would know exactly what you're talking about if you use the word 'whale' with an additional long 'e' syllable at the end.

Each letter in the Niuean alphabet has only one sound, and each sound is represented by only one letter. This makes learning to speak the language easy if you have the words written down to practise with.

Vowels

The five Niuean short vowels are pronounced much as they are in languages such as Spanish, German and Italian.

a	as the 'a' in 'father'
e	as the 'e' in 'bet'
i	as the 'ee' in 'see'
o	as the 'o' in 'more'
u	as the 'oo' in 'zoo'

Vowels with macrons such as ā, ē, ī, ō and ū indicate that the vowel is pronounced significantly longer than the corresponding unmarked vowel. An approximate English equivalent would be the difference between the final vowel sound in 'icy' and 'I see'. Niuen words also often have the same vowel side by side within a word, indicating that each is to be pronounced as its own syllable.

To get the correct pronunciation and meaning of a word, it's important that the length of the vowel sound is indicated. For example, mama means 'a ring', maama means 'to understand', and māmā means 'light (in weight)'.

Niueans themselves rarely, if ever, write macrons, since it wasn't part of the system of writing taught to them by missionaries, and in any case vowel length is often clear from context. On the other hand, macrons are essential for the language learner, and are used throughout this chapter.

When two vowels appear together, they retain their individual sounds, and can be pronounced as two separate syllables. However, with the speed of normal speech, they tend to be pronounced as one syllable as follows:

ai	as the 'y' in 'my'
au	as the 'ow' in 'now'
ei	as the 'ay' in 'lay'
oi	as the 'oy' in 'toy'
ou	as the 'oe' in 'hoe'
iu	as the 'ew' in 'few'

ATTRACTING ATTENTION

To attract someone's attention from a distance, use a loud sudden hiss accompanied by a beckoning gesture of a wave with the palm downwards. To attract the attention of someone sitting next to you, it's fine to whisper to them or touch them on the arm.

NIUEAN

Consonants

Most consonants are pronounced as they are in English, but a few differences need to be learned. There are 10 consonants in Niuean – f, g, h, k, l, m, n, p, t and v.

g	as the 'ng' in 'sing'
k	as in English, but without the following puff of breath
t	as the 's' in 'sing' when followed by è or i; elsewhere as the 't' in 'tar'

When English words are borrowed into Niuean, they're usually made to sound like Niuean ones.

b	changes to 'p' – 'bus' becomes pasi
d	changes to 't' – 'drum' becomes talam
q	changes to 'k' – 'quarter' becomes kuata
r	changes to 'l' when it's the first letter of a word – 'radio' becomes letio; may also be pronounced as in English
j	changes to 'i' or 'si' (pronounced *see*) – 'Jesus' becomes Iesu, 'John' becomes Sione
w	changes to 'u' – 'Willie' becomes Uili
ch	changes to 'k' or 's' – 'cheque' becomes sieke
th	changes to 't' or 'f' – 'Matthew' becomes Mataio, 'Timothy' becomes Timofi

Stress

Stress almost always falls on the second-last syllable. Words ending in a long vowel receive stress on the final syllable. Long vowels in other positions are given secondary stress.

Intonation

In most cases, the best way to learn Niuean intonation is simply to follow the intonation patterns of native speakers. Intonation is important in distinguishing between statements and yes/no questions since, unlike English, word order doesn't change for questions. Fortunately, the intonation for questions is similar to English – that is, with the pitch of the voice rising towards the end of the sentence. Thus, Kai! with low pitch throughout is a command for someone to eat, whereas Kai? with high rising pitch is a question meaning 'Would you like to eat?'.

MEETING PEOPLE
Greetings

The all-purpose greeting in Niue is Fakaalofa atu (lit: greetings to you). You can use it with everyone, in both formal and informal situations.

Hello. (to two people)	Fakaalofa atu ki a mua.
Hello. (to a group of people)	Fakaalofa atu ki a mutolu.
Hello. (to a large number of people, as when addressing a group)	Fakaalofa atu ki a mutolu oti.

In reply, you say the same back to them. It's common to ask someone how they're doing, Malolo nakai a koe? In reply, you should say Malolo, fakaaue (lit: healthy, thank you).

It's usual to greet anyone you encounter, either informally with Koe kia, or with the more elaborate Fakaalofa atu. People will also often ask where you've come from or where you're going. If you're in a hurry, smile and nod and point to where you're going.

NIUEAN

HANDSHAKES & KISSES

Shaking hands is standard practice between men, but women, even on first meeting, may greet each other with a kiss on the cheek. This is particularly the case in a formal situation, at church or when being introduced to an elderly woman. If you already know a Niuean and you haven't seen them for a while (even only a week), it's customary to kiss them on the cheek. A kiss on the cheek is standard goodbye protocol when leaving the island.

Where are you going?   Fano ki fe?
Nowhere in particular.   Ai fai.

Goodbyes
I'll be going now.   To fano au.
   Thanks. (in reply)   Fakaaue. (pol)
   Thanks. (in reply)   Ha ia. (inf)

Goodbye.   To feleveia.
                                         (lit: until we meet again).
   Goodbye. (in reply)   Ae. (inf)
   Goodbye. (in reply)   Fakaaue. (pol)
   Goodbye. (in reply)   To feleveia. (general)

I'll be back.   To lui mai au.
Thanks, that's it. (when   Fakaaue, toka pihia.
  ending a conversation)
Goodbye.   Fano ti malolo. (inf)
  (to someone leaving)
Goodbye.   Nofo ti malolo. (inf)
  (to someone staying behind)

Forms of Address
Niueans usually have more than one name – a palagi name (western-style name) and a Niuean name. They'll be more likely to tell you their palagi name, such as David, rather than ask you to call them Tevita. The best advice is to listen to what others say, or to ask.

NIUEAN TIME

A scheduled event may specifically say that it will start on palagi time, which refers to the time given. Niuean time is usually at least an hour later than the given time. It's acceptable to ask Matahola palagi po ke matahola fakaniue? meaning, 'Palagi time or Niuean time?'.

There are no formalities with Niuean names, so you don't have to worry about forms of address such as 'Mr' or 'Mrs'. When greeting an elder, if you don't know their name, call them matua.

Most people are commonly addressed by their first name. However, if you don't know their name, you can refer to their occupation.

teacher	faiaoga
minister (of religion)	faifeau
minister's wife	hoana ha faifeau
doctor	ekekafo
dentist	tagata taute nifo
policeman	leoleo

Body Language & Etiquette

Niueans convey agreement by an upward movement of the head or by raising the eyebrows.

The word Tulou is often used, sometimes when invading someone's personal space, such in a crowd, or when passing behind or in front of someone who's sitting down. When passing in front of someone, it's customary to crouch down a bit or, at the very least, lower your head while saying Tulou.

When visiting a village, swimsuits should be covered, and short-sleeved tops are preferable to sleeveless ones. It's impolite to wear shoes in a Niuean house. Leave them outside even if the host tells you it's OK to wear them indoors.

If you arrive at someone's home, they'll probably invite you to stay for the next meal or for a cup of tea. Fia inu ti? means 'Do you want a cup of tea?' and Inu ti will refer to anything from a cup of tea to a full meal.

NIUEAN

APOLOGIES

I'm sorry.	Tulou.
Don't worry.	Ai tupetupe.
That's OK.	Toka pihia.

If you want to politely decline the invitation, simply say Nakai, fakaue 'no, thanks'. This might not work and a Niuean will go through great lengths to prepare something anyway. It's best to say Kai tei au 'I've already eaten' if you don't want any food.

Family

aunt (mother's older sister)	matua taokete he matua fifine
aunt (mother's younger sister)	matua tehina he matua fifine
aunt (father's sister)	matua mahakitaga he matua taane
brother (female speaking)	tugaane
older brother (male speaking)	taokete
younger brother (male speaking)	tehina
children	tau fānau
cousin	matakainaga
daughter (lit: child girl)	tama fifine
daughter-in-law	figona fifine
family	magafaoa
father	matua taane
father-in-law	faimaā
grandfather	matua tupuna taane
grandmother	matua tupuna fifine
husband	taane
in-laws (together)	lafu maā
mother	matua fifine
mother-in-law	faimaā

NIUEAN

RESPONDING TO INVITATIONS

Thanks.	Fakaaue.
Thank you very much.	Fakaaue lahi mahaki.
No thanks.	Nakai, fakaaue.

REQUESTS

The usual way to broach a request is to begin by saying fakamolemole. After that, simply state what you want.

sister (male speaking)	mahakitaga
older sister (female speaking)	taokete
younger sister (female speaking)	tehina
son (lit: child boy)	tama taane
son-in-law	figona taane
uncle (father's older brother)	matua taokete he matua taane
uncle (father's younger brother)	matua tehina he matua taane
uncle (mother's brother)	matua tugaane he matua fifine
wife	hoana

NIUEAN

FORMING WORDS

In Niuean, complex words are made up of variations of a root word by using reduplication, suffixes and prefixes. When learning the language, this can be helpful as there are few root words to learn. It may take a while to get used to, but once you understand the primary prefixes and suffixes, you'll find it easier to express yourself even with only a handful of root words. For example, the word kite (to see; to understand) is partially reduplicated to create the word ki-kite (to look out). It's fully reduplicated to create kite-kite (to look carefully; to observe). A standard prefix creates faka-kite (to show). A suffix creates kite-aga (lesson/discovery). A final combination of a common prefix and suffix creates fe-kite-aki (to see each other).

FOOD

Eating without sharing is considered to be rude in Niue. If eating something like sweets, offer them to whoever you're with, perhaps saying Kai, 'eat'. If you see someone you know while you're eating a meal, it's customary to invite them to eat with you by saying Hau ke kai meaning 'come and eat'. Make an effort to pour a cup of tea or prepare a plate to give to your guest.

To excuse yourself from an offer of food, simply say Nakai, fakaaue, and say or point to where you're going. If you've already eaten, you can say Kai tei au or makona tei au

During meals, the host may say:

Kai ki makona.	Eat until you're full.
Makona?; Makona tei?	Are you full already?

When you've had enough, say:

Thanks a lot for the food!	Fakaaue lahi ke he kai!
I'm full, thanks.	Makona tei au, fakaaue.

A typical Niuean meal consists of two components – a boiled or earth-oven baked root vegetable, and fish or corned beef. Niueans eat taro with every nearly every meal, but kumara, bread fruit or cassava are also common substitutes.

Local Dishes

fai kai
> fish baked in the earth-oven with coconut cream

lū
> young taro leaves mixed with coconut cream and baked in the earth-oven

nane
> coconut juice, grated coconut and arrowroot powder

ota
> raw fish, usually wahoo, marinated in lime juice and served with coconut cream

pitako

grated banana or cassava baked with coconut cream

puaka

pork baked whole in the earth-oven

takihi

thinly sliced taro layered with pawpaw, covered with coconut cream and baked in the earth-oven

GETTING AROUND
Car

On the main highway, always be prepared for the unexpected, such as wandering livestock or children playing in the road.

If you're on foot, the chances are that someone will stop and ask you if you need a lift – with such a small population, Niueans usually know who the visitors are. It's not considered impolite to turn down an offer of a ride by saying Nakai fakaaue, fano au ke he evaeva meaning, 'no thank-you, I'm just walking around'. If you want to get the attention of an oncoming car, look at the driver and make a scooping signal with your arm, and with your palm down toward you.

NIUEAN

NIUEAN LITERATURE

Niue has a small community of poets and writers. Contemporary literature includes works by John Pule, the author of the novels *The Shark that Ate the Sun* and *Burn My Head in Heaven*. The Niue Writers Association has published *Musings on Niue*. Other notable books about Niue include *Niue: A History of the Island*, a collection of essays in Niuean and English by prominent Niueans that trace the history of the island, and *Would A Good Man Die?* by Dick Scott about the murder of the resident New Zealand High Commissioner on Niue, Cecil Larson. Niue also boasts an excellent Niuean–English dictionary, *Tohi Vagahau Niue*, for anyone serious about learning the Niuean language.

NIUEAN

In the Country

If you'd like to look around a village, it's OK to walk straight in and have a look around, but don't ignore people close by. Talk to someone and say Kua manako au ke kitia e maaga haau, 'I'd like to look around your village'. Even if one person waves you on, speak with others you see so they know you're a visitor.

Geographical Terms

bay	loto ava
beach	mataafaga
bridge	halalaupapa
cave	ana
earthquake	mafuike
farm	faama
forest	vaouhi
grassland	vao
harbour	ava
hill	palia
island	motu tu taha
jungle	uhi
lake	namo
mountain	mouga
mountain range	atu mouga
ocean	moana
pool (small pool on the reef)	loto
reef	uluulu
river	vailele
village	maaga
waterfall	vai tafe

NIUEAN SNAPSHOTS

Few Niueans have cameras, but most love having their picture taken. Photo development isn't always available on Niue, so a wonderful gesture is to take a lot of pictures of your Niuean friends and then mail them a copy after you leave.

Seasons

spring	vaha tau tupu (lit: season when things sprout)
summer	vaha mafana (lit: warm season)
autumn	vaha tau mateafu (lit: season when things die)
winter	vaha makalili (lit: cold season)

Souvenirs & Artefacts

bark cloth	hiapo
club	katoua
earrings	tifa
garland	kahoa
grass skirt	titi
handicraft	koloa motu; tufuga lima
mats	potu
necklace	monomono
ring	mama
shells	tifa
wood carvings	tiki

NIUEAN

CELEBRATIONS

There are many celebrations in Niue, reflecting the mix of traditional cultural influences and modern day events. For Niueans, Christmas and Easter are celebrated, but essentially as religious festivals.

initiation ceremonies

Niuean children have a ceremony that celebrates their transition into adulthood. Traditionally, these ceremonies were only for the eldest child, but these days, every child usually gets his or her chance. Boys let their hair grow until their hifi ulu (hair cutting) ceremony, which may be held anytime between the ages of five and 18. Until a boy gets his hair cut, he's likely to wear it in a single braid down his back. During a hair cutting, the boy's hair is braided into many tiny braids. Each honoured guest gets to cut off and keep one of the braids.

During the hukiteliga ceremony, girls have their ears pierced. A girl's grandmothers have the honour of piercing her ears. This is often done traditionally with a thorn from the lime tree (foto tipolo), but nowadays it's also common for piercing to be done with a modern piercer.

If you're at an ear-piercing ceremony, it's best to introduce yourself to the family before you show up, or otherwise watch the ceremony from the outside. If you want a seat up front, introduce yourself to someone and let them know, and you'll probably be accommodated. If you want to sit up close, you should dress appropriately – women wear dresses and men wear long pants and collared shirts.

Peniamina's Day

Peniamina is the Niuean who first brought Christianity to Niue. Peniamina's Day in October is a Niuean holiday and offers a range of activities from golf tournaments to dance festivals. Niue has been self-governing since 1974 and annual constitution celebrations are usually held in conjunction with Peniamina's Day

Prayer Week

the Niuean New Year begins at church. Often people will go out until 11 pm on New Year's Eve, leave to go to church at midnight, then back out to the clubs to dance until the sun comes up. Typically, clubs close at midnight, but on New Year's Eve they're open past 2 am.

The first week of the New Year begins each morning with church. Typically, all members of the village will participate during at least one day, either by reading from the Bible or by saying a prayer. Each day has a different theme, from praying for the children to praying for the government.

takai

at the end of Prayer Week, each village organises a takai, which basically involves a parade around the island. Niue is only about 56km in circumference and the trip takes several hours. People decorate their cars, trucks and motorcycles with coconut fronds, flower garlands, balloons and flags. As the takai goes through each village, it's customary to toss sweets to those waiting by the road. There's usually one stop for lunch or for a swim on the takai. Once the takai is finished, the villagers get together for a picnic or barbecue, and party for the rest of the day and night.

NIUEAN

TIME & DATES
Days

Monday	Aho Gofua
Tuesday	Aho Ua
Wednesday	Aho Lotu
Thursday	Aho Tuloto
Friday	Aho Falaile
Saturday	Aho Faiumu
Sunday	Aho Tapu

MOUI HOHOKO!

If someone sneezes, say Moui hohoko! The reply is tuputiola (bless you).

Months

January	Ianuali	July	Iulai
February	Fepuali	August	Aokuso
March	Mati	September	Sepetema
April	Apelila	October	Oketopa
May	Me	November	Novema
June	Iuni	December	Tesemo

SONG: FAREWELL SONG

This is a popular song sung to people
leaving the island.

Kapitiga fano a koe
  My friend, you are leaving
Nofo au mo e tagi
  I stay and cry
He iloa e hai
  Who knows
Ato liu fekiteaki
  when you'll return and we'll meet again
Oi Aue! he mamao e moana
  Oh! Far across the ocean
Nakai galo e au a koe
  Don't you forget me
Fano ti manatu mai
  Go, but think of me

Toe Hifo au hinei
  I'm left down here on this place
Ha ko e tau matagahua
  What can I do
Ne kotofa e ia au ke fekafekau
  for you to choose me to serve you?
Oi Aue! he mameo e moana
  Oh! Far across the ocean
Nakai galo e au a koe
  Don't you forget me
Fano ti manatu mai
  Go, but think of me

NUMBERS

0	nakai
1	taha
2	ua
3	tolu
4	fa
5	lima
6	ono
7	fitu
8	valu
9	hiva
10	hogofulu
11	hogofulu ma taha
12	hogofulu ma ua
13	hogofulu ma tolu
14	hogofulu ma fa
15	hogofulu ma lima
16	hogofulu ma ono
17	hogofulu ma fitu
18	hogofulu ma valu
19	hogofulu ma hiva

NIUEAN

NIUEAN NAMES

If you'd like to 'Niueanise' your name, here are some common equivalents.

Beth	Peta
Jane	Seini
John	Sione
Mary	Mele
Paul	Paulo
Peter	Pita
Rose	Losa
Timothy	Timofi

NIUEAN

20	uafulu
21	uafulu ma taha
22	uafulu ma ua
30	tolugofulu
31	tolugofulu ma taha
40	fagofulu
50	limagofulu
60	onogofulu
70	fitugofulu
80	valugofulu
90	hivagofulu
100	taha e teau
101	taha e teau taha
102	taha e teau ua
193	taha e teau hivagofulu ma tolu
200	ua e teau
300	tolu e teau
400	fa e teua
500	lima e teau
600	ono e teau
700	fitu e teau
800	valu e teau
900	hiva e teau
1000	taha e afe
2000	ua e afe

WEIGHT NOT TABOO

Weight as a subject isn't taboo in Niue. If you're heavy, Niueans mean no offence, but may come out and say, in English, 'you're fat!'.

RAPANUI

EASTER ISLAND (RAPA NUI)

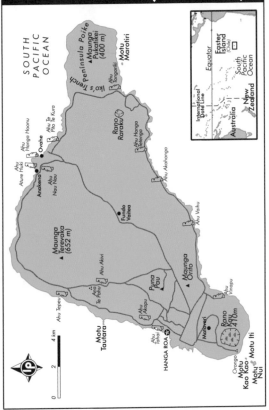

INTRODUCTION

> Ku hanga 'ā qu mo oho ki 'a Rapa Nui.
> I want to go to Rapa Nui.

Spanish is the official language of Easter Island, used in commerce, education and government since Chile annexed Easter Island in 1888. Thus at the airport, bank, hospital or any government-run operation, the language used will be Spanish (see page *** for a basic introduction to Spanish). In addition, some Rapanui Islanders – especially tour guides and hotel staff – can speak passable English, German or French.

Although Rapanui islanders speak Spanish, many also speak among themselves in Rapanui. Saying things like 'please', 'thank you', 'hello' and, of course, 'to your health!' in the language of the islanders will be appreciated. Or you may have an interest in the Rapanui language and its relationship to other languages in Polynesia, or may like to convince others that the Rapanui language should be preserved and studied. Most importantly, the Rapanui islanders will be pleased that you're attempting to speak their language, and it's a great way to make island friends.

As is the case for all languages, and especially those spoken by small groups of people (there are fewer than 4000 Rapanui world-wide), the Rapanui tongue is being influenced by the outside world. Many of the words used today are Tahitian in origin. Some Rapanui words may seem familiar, as many words have been borrowed from English and Spanish. Of course, words for relatively recent inventions like 'automobile', 'television' and 'aeroplane' have also entered the language.

Sadly, many of the younger Islanders know only a smattering of their unique native language. Most understand Rapanui, but few can speak it fluently. However, Rapanui is now being taught at the island school. Much of the past history and ethnology of the ancient people are tied up in the words and legends. Knowing that their early ancestors spoke a fully developed and highly sophisticated language provides Rapanui people with the incentive and pride necessary to prevent their language from disappearing.

In the 19th century, missionaries transliterated the sounds of the Rapanui language into the Roman alphabet. Thus on the island you may see signs or posters written in Rapanui. Some textbooks exist, as do a number of storybooks and written poetry. Portions of scripture have been translated into Rapanui since the 1860s.

History

The Rapanui language is an Austronesian language that originally came out of South-east Asia and has been evolving over the past millennia. Because of Easter Island's isolation, the Rapanui language that was spoken when the first Westerners arrived – thought to be the Dutch in 1722 – was untouched by outside influence. Unlike inhabited islands to the west, there was no interchange of words and phrases taking place as one island group visited another. However, when Captain Cook arrived in 1774, the Tahitian crew that Cook brought along could understand much of the language – it was, after all, a Polynesian language. Although most Rapanui words are similar to the corresponding ones used by the indigenous people of Tahiti, Samoa, New Zealand and the Cook and the Hawaiian Islands, others are entirely different – Rapanui is a distinct language and not a dialect.

PRONUNCIATION

The pronunciation of Rapanui words is easy, especially if you know a little Italian or Spanish. If you remember to pronounce every letter using a latino accent, you'll come close to having a Rapanui accent. For example, the Rapanui word for the creator god is Makemake and is pronounced something like *maa-kay maa-kay* – not to rhyme with 'cake bake'.

The apostrophe mark (') that you'll often see in Rapanui signifies a glottal stop (like the sound made between the words in 'uh-oh'). Thus the word ra'ā, meaning 'sun', has two syllables, with a definite break between the two.

There are 15 letters in Rapanui, or 20 when you include long vowels. If you read or hear a word that has other letters, you'll know that the word is not native Rapanui, such as sau sau, which is Samoan for 'feast' or 'fiesta'. And even though the letter 'b' doesn't exist in the Rapanui alphabet, a bicycle is called a bicycle almost anywhere in the world.

Vowels

a   as the 'a' in 'father'
e   somewhere between the 'ay' in 'hay' and the 'e' in 'bet'
i   as the 'ee' in 'see'
o   as the 'o' in 'hot'
u   as the 'oo' in 'boot'

At times you'll see a line over a vowel, as in ā, ē, ī, ō and ū. This is called a macron and is used in Pacific island languages to indicate that the vowel is longer than the equivalent unmarked vowel. The length of the vowel can change the meaning of a word. The Rapanui seldom use macrons when they write because they already know which vowels are long, but macrons are helpful for the beginner who's learning pronunciation.

Diphthongs are easily spotted in Rapanui text. The three most common diphthongs are:

ai   as the 'y' in 'sky'
au   like the 'ow' in 'cow'
oi   like the 'oy' in 'toy'

Consonants

The sound of Rapanui can be soft, fluid and melodic, without many of the hard sounds heard in European languages. There are only ten consonants in Rapanui – h, k, m, n, p, r, t, v, ng and the glottal stop ('), which sound like the sound made between the words in 'uh-oh'. When n and g appear together, ng is pronounced as the ng in 'sing' and not as in 'finger'. (In some books you'll see the ng written as ŋ.) These consonants, including ng, sound much like their English equivalents.

Stress

Most words in Rapanui take stress on the second-last syllable, which is often slightly lengthened. Stress can also be placed on a vowel with a macron (such as ā) when it appears at the end of a word.

MEETING PEOPLE
Greetings & Goodbyes

Hello.	'Iorana. (pronounced *ee-yore-raa-na*)
Goodbye.	'Iorana.
	Ku mao 'ā. (old Rapanui)
How are you (sg/pl)?	Pehē koe/kōrua?
Fine.	Rivariva.
What's your name?	Ko āi to'ou ingoa?
My name's ...	To'oku ingoa ko ...

Family

Many of the terms now used for family members are based on the Spanish names. For example, mamatia and papatio are now used for aunt and uncle, whereas in old Rapanui, matu'a kē was used for aunts, uncles and relatives in general.

aunt	mamatia
brother	ta'ina tāne
cousin	ta'ina kē
father	matu'a
daughter	pōki vahine
grandchild	makupuna
grandparent	rū'au

RAPANUI

RAPANUI HISTORY

A written account of Rapanui history handed down through oral tradition can be found in *Island at the Center of the World*, written by Sebastian Englert.

husband	kenu
mother	nua
relative	ere
sibling	ere
sister	ta'ina vahine
son	pōki tāne
uncle	papatio
wife	vī'e/vahine

People & Gods

baby	pōki
boy	pōki tāne
chief	'ariki
children	ngāpōki
friend	ngaruhoa
girl	pōki vahine
ghost	akuaku
god	'atua
god of creation	Makemake
king	'ariki
man	tāne/tangata
police	mūto'i
priest	'oromatu'a
woman	vī'e/vahine
young person	kope

RAPANUI

FOOD

Island specialties on Rapa Nui are fish (naturally) and chicken, but meat (beef or pork) is also common. Vegetables include sweet potato, taro root, salad, and that Polynesian delicacy, po'i (baked and fermented taro).

By all means, try to get yourself invited to a first-rate 'umu, the island's special cook-out. All these foods will probably be included on the menu. The po'i on Rapa Nui differs from the kind normally served in Hawaii in that it's cooked, usually with bananas, and has a cake-like texture. Delicious!

There are many different kinds of fish available on Rapa Nui (around 90 species). The favorite types of fish are kahi (tuna) and nanue (rudderfish). Kahi is caught from the small fishing boats that go out from the caleta (a small bay that lies at the foot of the village), while nanue is caught with fishing line cast from the rocky coastline.

Meat, Fish & Fowl

beef	kiko
chicken	moa
(raw) fish	ika (mata)
ham	hūhā
lobster	'ura/kō'ura
pork	oru o'otu
rudderfish	nanue
shark	mangō
sole	rahai
tuna	kahi

Fruit

banana	maika
guava (quince)	tuava
orange	'ānani
papaya	'ī'ītā
pineapple	ananā
tomato	tōmāti
watermelon	marēni

Vegetables

beans	arikō
lettuce	pota
onion	'oniāna
potato	kumā
salad	sara
taro	taro

At the Market

There are many stores on Rapa Nui, and some carry such things as pāreu (skirt or loincloth) from Tahiti and locally made artefacts of wood or stone, which are copies of ancient pieces. Shell necklaces are popular and may contain shells from Tahiti as well as from Easter Island.

How much does this cost?	'Ehia moni o te me'e nei?

GETTING AROUND

Rapa Nui is small, a little over 11km by 24km (7 by 15 miles), and today there's only one village on the island, although this wasn't the case in ancient times. Since the days of the early sheep ranches, islanders have lived at Hanga Roa, on the west side of the island. Today this town has the only electricity, water and telephone services, gas station, and so on. As it isn't a large town, getting around the village is relatively simple. The airport is just south of town. The stores, the school, the soccer field, the Church, government services and nearly all the hotels are in or near the town centre. About the only thing that starts on time is the service at the Catholic church.

Although taxis are available, there's no bus service. Most visitors to the island rent a vehicle – the advantage of renting a car is that you can take shelter in it when a rainstorm rolls in over the island. Some visitors go on organised tours and some rent a horse. Horseback is a good way to get around, provided you don't end up with a nag (or one that's half wild).

RAPANUI

Sightseeing

If you have limitless time, walking can be a fine way to see the island and its archaeological sites. However, it's a long way from the village to many of the places you might want to see. The most outstanding sites include the famous statues, mōai (see page 150). Ahu (shrines, see page 148) are found all over the island, but mainly along the coast, and there are also many other ancient Rapanui structures or artefacts.

ahu	ceremonial structure; platform
avanga	burial cave; niche
hare moa	chicken house; tombs
hare pa'enga	boat-shaped house; status dwelling
kaikai	string-figure game
keho	stone slabs used to build houses at 'Orongo
koro	feast to honour an adult
manavai	circular structures made for the protection of plants
mara'e	sacred place surrounded by a low wall
mōai	statue
pa'enga	cut stone blocks of dense basalt
pa'epa'e	small house; shack
paina	stone circles in front of ahu where koro were held
pipihoreko	tower made of stone which marks a boundary
pora	float made of totora reeds
poro	beach cobbles, used to form ramps at ahu
pukao	stone 'hats' for statues
taheta	basin made of carved stone
tūpa	hollow stone structure
'umu	earth oven

Souvenirs & Artefacts

'ao	ceremonial staff
kavakava	sculpture of emaciated figure
korone	necklace

RAPANUI

mahute	barkcloth
mata'a	spearhead made of hard black obsidian (volcanic rock)
mōai ma'ea	statue (stone)
mōai miro	statue (wooden)
pipi	shells (small, decorative)
pukao	topknot or crown
rapa	dance paddle
reimiro	chest ornament in a crescent-shape
rongorongo	tablet with incised figures
tahonga	pendant (stone or wooden)
tangata manu	birdman
toki	stone adze, used as a tool to carve moai
totora	reed vessel
tuitui	collar
ua	ceremonial wooden staff with two faces

Geographical Terms

Two good swimming beaches are on the opposite side of the island from the village, as is the famous statue quarry Rano Raraku

DID YOU KNOW ... Kavakava, 'statues of ribs', are the wooden figures carved on Rapa Nui which feature hollow cheeks, sunken abdomens and protruding ribs. According to oral tradition, King Tuu-ko-ihu came across two aku aku (sleeping ghosts) who were so thin their ribs stood out. Tuu-ko-ihu quickly carved their likeness in wood before he forgot their appearance, and since then islanders have always carved these statues.

RAPANUI

bay	hanga
beach	tahatai
boat	vaka
canoe	vaka
cave	'ana
crater	rano
division of land; family land	kāinga
earth	henua
fence	'aua
flat area of lava	papa
fire	ahi
harbour	hanga
hill	ma'unga
hole	pū
house	hare
lake	rano
land	henua
moon	mahina
mountain	ma'unga
ocean	vai kava
sand	'one
star	hetu'u

AHU

About 245 ahu line much of Easter Island's coast. Each ahu is a mass of loose stones held together by retaining walls and paved on the upper surface. There's usually a wall at each end and facing the sea, and a ramp on the side facing land.

Ahu were used as burial sites, and the moai (see page 150) sometimes positioned on them may have represented clan ancestors. Stone-lined ramps leading into the sea by the side of some ahu were used to launch canoes.

tree	tumu
wall	'aua
water	vai
water hole	pū

Weather

Although there's no word in Rapanui for 'weather', there are many descriptive words for the winds. The winds are named according to the direction from which they blow toward the centre of the island. There are also no words for the four seasons, undoubtedly because there's no marked distinction between spring and summer or autumn and winter.

autumn/winter	tonga
blow fiercely	hūhū
breeze	hahau
cloud	rangi
hard rain	'ua mata varavara
rain	'ua
sky	rangi
spring/summer	hora
sun	ra'ā
wind	tokerau
north wind	te pakakina
south wind	puhi 'a 'orongo
east wind	ko roto o niu
west wind	ko motu takarua me'a

RAPANUI

QUESTION WORDS	
What?	Aha?
Which?	Hē aha?
Who?	Ko āi?
Of whom?	'A āi?
For whom?	Mo āi?

Fauna & Flora

Before missionaries arrived, the only animals on the island were chickens, which had made the long sea voyage with Rapa Nui's first settlers, and rats. Most animals have been introduced and have names taken from Spanish or English. Many plants were already known and some arrived with the first settlers, along with insects and lizards. The Rapanui had names for migratory sea birds, but recent additions of some bird species from Chile have been given Rapanui names – some of which are quite descriptive. Sea creatures include many kinds of fish, lobster and, in ancient times, turtles, which are rare today.

Birds

bird	manu
chicken	moa
frigate bird	makohe

RAPANUI

DID YOU KNOW ... Carved from hard volcanic tuff, moai statues feature elongated, rectangular heads with heavy brows and prominent chins, protruding abdomens and long, slender fingers. Although all moai are similar, few are identical, and they can vary in height from two metres to just under 21 metres.

The only moai standing today have been restored to upright position this century. Moai belonging to rival clans are thought to have been toppled during intertribal warfare as a means of insulting an enemy.

partridge	vīvī
tropic bird	tavake
sooty tern	manutara
sparrow hawk	manu toketoke
	(lit: bird that steals)

Mammals

bull	puāa tāne
cat	kurī
cow	puāa vahine
dog	paihenga
horse	hoi
rat	kio'e

Sea Creatures

crab	pikea
fish	ika
lobster	kō'ura
octopus	heke
rudderfish	nanue
shark	mangō
tuna	kahi
turtle	hōnu

Plants

flower	tiare/pua
fruit tree	tumu kai
grass	maūku
leaf	raupā
palm tree	niu
tree	miro
tree trunk	tumu
tree indigenous to Rapa Nui	(sophora) toromiro
wood	miro

RAPANUI

FESTIVALS
Dia de Independencia

The official Chilean holiday on 18 September that celebrates national independence is also observed on Easter Island. Festivities include races and a parade in which every islander with a uniform, including school children, participates. Parties are held at the fonda – a cluster of food and drink stands where there's loud music and some games of chance – set up near the caleta especially for this occasion.

Tapati Rapanui

Tapati, a two-week festival of dance, song, performance and general festivities, begins at the end of January or early February. Tapati began in 1975. Back then, it was a song and poetry festival. Today's productions feature native dance, chants, song, horse racing, woodcarving, fishing, kai kai (string figures), traditional body decoration and a parade.

Tapati occurs at the height of summer, so although dance and song performances are generally held in the island's gymnasium, many are also held out of doors in front of one or another of the great ahu platforms, such as at Tongariki or Tahai. Some of these performances are more like dance-drama, such as the recreation of the first landing of Hotu Matu'a (see page 155), enacted at Anakena or Ovahe beach by torchlight.

DID YOU KNOW ... The topknots that were placed on many moai statues, called pukao, are thought to reflect a common hairstyle worn by Rapa Nui men. Most pukao had a clearly marked knot on the top and were partly hollowed out underneath so they could fit onto the moai heads.

Since the filming of a Hollywood movie on the island in 1993, the festival events have become more sophisticated. This is particularly evident in the parade that's held near the end of the festival. The parade features decorated floats, each bearing a 'queen' contestant, accompanied by supporters dressed in native costumes who sing and dance by torchlight along the parade route.

The crowning of the queen is always a big event – the competition is very fierce and pits family against family. The queens amass points from the competitors – to whom they're usually related – who compete in their name. Thus the contests take on a social aspect as well as giving status within the community. The queen is crowned on the last Saturday night of the festival. But the following night, there's an impromptu alfresco crowning held at the nearby archaeological site of Tahai where, by moonlight and torchlight, another crown is placed on her head.

Sporting events are based on ancient games and activities. Haka pei involves sliding down a steep hillside on the trunk of a banana tree, wearing little more than a hami (loincloth) and body paint. The contestant who stays on his log to the bottom of the hill and who goes the farthest is the winner. This suicidal competition has to be seen to be believed.

Another unusual event is a triathlon-type contest that involves paddling on totora reed bundles across the lake at Rano Raraku, followed by a race around the lake carrying a pole with huge banana clusters at each end across the shoulders. All this is done barefoot and in the usual hami with body paint.

Recently, other ancient skills have been added to the competition. These include making mahute (barkcloth), chipping obsidian to make mata'a (stone tools), a shell necklace-making contest, and a competition to make the best stone statue within a set time .

Others compete for the best display of family grown, local vegetables and fruits. There's also a display of wood carvings and an exhibition of work from local painters and photographers.

Dance competitions include the usual sexy Polynesian dancing as well as a children's night, a contest for older islanders and dancing competitions that feature more modern music.

RAPANUI

Aside from the contest activities, Tapati is generally a time for partying. With dances and parties, the actual festival program and discos open until morning, little other work gets done.

Christmas

On Easter Island, Christmas is a religious holiday, with very little of the commercialism so rampant in many other cultures. What seems like the entire population crowds into the church for midnight Mass and a pageant depicting the nativity.

BIRDMAN

Makemake, the birdman cult's supreme deity, was said to have created the earth, sun, moon, stars and people. He rewarded good and punished evil.

Followers of the cult are thought to have periodically gone to Orongo to pray, make offerings and hold rites to appease the gods. The climax of their ceremonies was a competition to find the first egg of the sooty tern, which bred on the tiny islets of Motu Nui, Motu Iti and Motu Kao Kao, just off Cabo te Manga. Contestants would descend the cliff from Orongo and swim out to the islands – the first person to find the first egg laid on the island became birdman for the ensuing year, winning both community status and Makemake's favour.

The winner's head, eyebrows and eyelashes were shaved, his face painted red and black, and, as birdman, he was sequestered in a specially appointed house. The last birdman ceremony took place at Orongo in 1866 or 1867.

LEGENDS

The drastic reduction of the population of Easter Island due to slave raids and epidemics in the late 1800s has meant there's little information about the past. A few legends were collected by Alfred Métraux (1940) and Katherine Routledge (1919), but these mainly deal with the settlement of the island, intertribal warfare and rivalry. Some stories touch on the mana of kings and the rongorongo script (see page 155), and the events that surrounded the birdman cult (see page 154).

Hoto Matu'a

The first immigrants to the island are said to have come from Marae-renga, an island to the west of Rapa Nui. The legend describes six men who landed prior to king Hotu Matu'a (matu'a meaning 'father') as a sort of reconnaissance, and one version mentions the canoes being at sea for two months. Oral tradition records 57 generations of kings succeeding Hotu Matu'a, which by some estimates would date his arrival at around 450 AD.

RONGORONGO TABLETS

At the time of early European contact, every house on Easter Island was said to contain wooden tablets covered in the rongorongo script. The tablets were flat wooden boards which were covered in rows of symbols that included birds, animals and geometric forms, representing whole words and repetitive phrases.

Oral tradition describes three types of tablet. One recorded hymns in honour of the god Makemake, another type recorded crimes committed by the islanders, while the third commemorated those who died in war.

Rongorongo has never been translated, and the last islanders literate in the script were either kidnapped or died of disease. It's thought that rongorongo might represent a series of cues for reciting memorised verse, or may be ideographs like Chinese script. Only a few of the tablets survive.

RAPANUI

Hotu Matu'a is credited with bringing cultivated plants and all land animals known to the natives (namely chickens), and with possessing the knowledge of the written language (rongorongo). It's said that he brought 67 rongorongo tablets with him.

Legends of Clan Warfare

The most frequently told legend is that of the battle of Poike ditch, called 'the war between the long ears and the short ears'. This legend has appeared in practically everything written about the island. While there's little doubt that wars and battles went on for much of the island's history, this legend has no basis in fact and was probably created to explain a natural feature in the landscape.

The story of the battle concerns a ruling group, called the hanau e'epe 'long ears', who ordered the hanau momoko 'short ears' to clear all the rocks off Poike. The short ears rebelled and, in a battle, all but one of the long ears were slaughtered and burned in a trench, the Poike ditch. But, because of its geological formation, there never were rocks on Poike, and the ditch is a natural earth slippage where two volcanoes came together.

The name hanau e'epe actually means 'fat people' and hanau momoko means 'thin people' – neither has anything to do with ears. Despite numerous excavations by archaeologists, nothing has ever been found in the ditch that would indicate that a battle took place, such as spear points, bones or artefacts.

RAPANUI

DEMONSTRATIVES

this one	te me'e nei
that one (nearby)	te me'e ena
that one (over there)	te me'e ēra
these ones	te ngā me'e nei
those (nearby)	te ngā me'e ena
those (over there)	te ngā me'e ēra

The Fallen Statues

Another legend is often told on the island to explain why the moai statues fell. It concerns a woman who was a sorcerer – she cooked lobster in an earth oven for the workers in the quarry, but cautioned them to save some for her. They ignored her request and ate everything. She was enraged and ordered all of the statues to fall.

TIME & DATES

Names for the days of the week have been introduced under Western influence – the ancient Rapanui words are the nights of the lunar calendar. Note that the old names (ra'ā pō + the number of the day) translate as 'night one' and so on.

Days   Mahana o te tāpati

	Modern Rapanui	Old Rapanui
Monday	monirē	ra'ā pō tahi
Tuesday	mahana piti	ra'ā pō rua
Wednesday	mahana toru	ra'ā pō toru
Thursday	mahana māha	ra'ā pō hā
Friday	mahana pae	ra'ā pō rima
Saturday	mahana hopu	ra'ā pō ono
Sunday	mahana tāpati	ra'ā pō hitu

RAPANUI

PLURALS

Nouns are usually made plural by placing ngā before the noun.

trees	ngā tumu

If a specific number is mentioned, ngā is omitted.

five trees	erima tumu

Months

Rapanui has two names for the months of the year, one modern and one used in ancient times.

	Modern Rapanui	Old Rapanui
January	senuari	tuaharo
February	februari	te hetu'u'pū
March	mati	tarahau
April	apirira	vaitūnui
May	mee	vaitūpotu
June	tiun	te maro
July	tiurai	'anakena
August	atete	hora 'iti
September	tetepa	hora nui
October	otopa	tangaroa 'uri
November	noema	koruti
December	titema	kokoro

NUMBERS
Cardinal Numbers

In Rapanui, there are two forms of cardinal numbers. The first, with the prefix 'e-, are used with nouns.

1	'etahi
2	'erua
3	'etoru

PRONOUNS

I	ko au
you (sg)	ko koe
he/she/it	ko ia
we (me and you)	ko tāua
we (me and others)	ko maua
you (pl)	ko korua
they	ko rā'ua

RAPANUI

4	'ehā
5	'erima
6	'eono
7	'ehitu
8	'eva'u
9	'eiva
10	'e'angahuru

three children	'etoru pōki
five statues	'erima mōai

For simple counting, the 'e- is replaced with ka-.

1	katahi
2	karua
3	katoru

Larger numbers get more complicated (for example, 15 is ehō'ē'ahuru ma pae), so we'll stop here except to note that one hundred is hānere and one thousand is pīere.

Ordinal Numbers

Except for 'first', ordinal numbers are the stems of the cardinal numbers preceded by te.

1st	te ra'e
2nd	te rua
3rd	te toru

RAPANUI

DID YOU KNOW ...	At Ahu Tahai, foundations still remain of hare paenga, traditional thatched houses built in the shape of an ellipse that resembled an upturned canoe. The larger ones could house more than 100 people.

TE PITO TE KURA

The largest moai ever moved from Rano Raraku (the statue quarry) was erected at on Ahu te Pito Kura. Nearby the fallen statue lies a large, round boulder that's often called 'the navel of the island'. Legend says Hotu Matu'a brought it from the ancient homeland, but the stone is actually a beach cobble formed of local rock.

4th	te hā
5th	te rima
6th	te ono
7th	te hitu
8th	te va'u
9th	te iva
10th	te katahi te 'angahuru
the third man	te toru tangata
the fifth horse	te rima hoi

When referring to the 'first', use only ra'e and put it after the noun.

the first man	tangata ra'e
the first hill	ma'unga ra'e

RAPANUI

RAROTONGAN MAORI

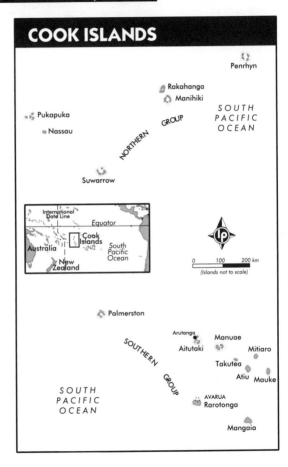

COOK ISLANDS

Penrhyn

Rakahanga
Manihiki

SOUTH
PACIFIC
OCEAN

Pukapuka

Nassau

NORTHERN GROUP

Suwarrow

International
Date Line

Equator

Australia

Cook
Islands
(NZ)

South
Pacific
Ocean

New
Zealand

0   100   200 km
(Islands not to scale)

Palmerston

SOUTHERN GROUP

Arutanga
Aitutaki

Manuae

Mitiaro

Takutea

Atiu   Mauke

AVARUA
Rarotonga

SOUTH
PACIFIC
OCEAN

Mangaia

RAROTONGAN MAORI

INTRODUCTION

Rarotongan Maori is actually a dialect of Cook Island Maori – one of 11 such dialects spoken in the Cook Islands. Because Rarotonga was the centre of missionary activities and government administration in the Cook Islands, the Rarotongan dialect has become the lingua franca of the Cook Islands. People on the outer islands speak their own dialects, but when communicating with visitors from Rarotonga or from another island in the group, they can easily switch to the Rarotongan dialect or to the other island dialect. Usually the visitor takes up the local dialect as a mark of respect and an expression of 'I feel at home already'. Cook Islanders also speak English, which is the language used in education.

Of the 15 islands that make up the Cook Islands, only 12 have been permanaently settled, and two of these islands use the same dialect. Of the three remaining islands, Suwarrow, named after a Russian ship, was made famous by the adventurer Tom Neale, who was its only inhabitant for years, Takutea is a bird sanctuary and Manuae is an unofficial marine reserve.

Rarotongan Maori was first written by missionaries in the 1830s, when it began to be used as the language of instruction. By the 1880s, the Bible was translated into Rarotongan.

PRONUNCIATION

Rarotongan Maori has five short vowels (a, e, i, o and u), and five long vowels (ā, ē, ī, ō and ū), which are pronounced significantly longer than the corresponding unmarked vowel. There are nine consonants (ng, k, m, n, p, r, t, v and the glottal stop (')). Each letter represents just one sound. All the consonants are exactly the same as in English, with the exception of r, which is pronounced with greater emphasis. The ng at the beginning of a word is usually a difficult one to get around. To help overcome that difficulty, simply say the word 'sing' and hold on with extreme concentration to the 'ng'. The glottal stop (') is the sound you make in between the words in 'uh-oh'.

MEETING PEOPLE

Rarotonga has been described as a paradise, not just for its climate and natural beauty, but also for its people. Although Cook Islands people are generally friendly, they can be very shy and most prefer to stay out of the limelight. They're naturally polite, however, and any visitor is made to feel at home the moment their hosts have overcome their shyness. There's no better way for the visitor to help achieve this than to say with a smile Kia orana, 'Hi' (lit: may life continue with you).

When invited to stay in a private home, it's polite to take something like chocolate or biscuits as a token of gratitude and friendship. Meitaki ma'ata no te takinga meitaki means 'Thank you for your hospitality'.

Greetings & Goodbyes

Good morning.	Kia orana 'i teia popongi.
Good day.	Kia orana 'i teia ra.
Peace.	Kia 'au!
Good evening.	Kia orana 'i teia a'ia'i.
Good night.	Night. This is the most common way to say goodnight, and is almost sung – N-i-i-i-g-h-t!
Goodbye. (to someone leaving)	'Aere ra.
Goodbye. (to someone staying behind)	'E no'o ra.
See you later.	Ka kite 'aka'ou a konei atu.
Have a good trip.	'Aere kia manuia.

Family

Ariki, mataiapo and rangatira is the ancient system of chiefs which has survived for centuries in an unbroken lineage. Rarotonga's six ariki clans are still based on the original land divisions that have survived from when the Maori first arrived on the island centuries ago. Every native Cook Islander is part of a family clan, and each family clan is connected in some distinct way to this system.

boyfriend	taeake tane
clan	ngati
daughter	tamāine
mother	mama
father	papa
girlfriend	taeake va'ine
husband	tane
older sister	tua'ine
older brother	tuakana
younger brother	teina
wife	va'ine
son	tamāroa

Gods & People

ariki	chief; traditional head of a tribe
Atua	God
mataiapo	head of sub-tribe, one rank down from an ariki
papa'a	foreigners
rangatira	landed gentry; lowest rank of Cook Islands royal hierarchy, below mataiapo
Tangaroa	traditional god of the sea and of fertility, this is the squat, ugly but well-endowed figure you find on the Cook Islands' one-dollar coin. Tangaroa has become the symbol of the Cook Islands, surviving early missionary attempts to wipe out all traditional gods.
taunga	expert

WHO'S THAT PLACE?

In the Cook Islands, names are considered to be living entities, so when asking about a place, Cook Islanders use ko 'ai 'who' instead of 'what'.

RAROTONGAN MAORI

FOOD
The Umu

Traditionally, Cook Islanders sit cross-legged on the floor, with food placed on banana leaves. Cooking is done in an earth oven called an umu, which is a round hole about half a metre in diameter and a third of a metre deep. The hole is filled with firewood, basalt rocks are piled on top and then the umu is lit. As the wood burns, the rocks become white hot and sink to the bottom. Left-over bits of charcoal and wood are removed, and the stones are spread on the bottom with a long stick and covered with strips of a banana trunk to keep the food from coming into direct contact with the hot stones. Food is then placed in the umu and covered with banana and/or breadfruit leaves. The leaves are then covered with sacks, and finally soil is thrown over to prevent the heat and steam from escaping too quickly.

About three hours later, depending on how hot the oven is, the cover is gently taken off and the food removed and prepared.

Umukai

A big feast is called an umukai, literally meaning 'food from the oven'. For an umukai, a large umu is dug and meat is cooked.

Each week, hotels hold an island night featuring island food, dancing, singing and an invitation for visitors to join in the dance. When you're invited to a party or umukai, dress is usually 'island style', which doesn't mean the style of dress used before the missionaries arrived – it means casual wear. For formal events, men wear a shirt and tie and shoes, and women a dress.

HE, SHE, IT, HIM, HER

Rarotongan Maori doesn't differentiatie between 'he', 'she', 'it', 'him' and 'her' – they're all expressed by aia. You'll often hear Cook Islanders mix up English pronouns to express what they have only one word for, calling men 'she' and women 'he'.

Local Dishes

kava

drink prepared from the root of the pepper plant. Non-alcoholic, but can cause anything from a mildly fuzzy head to total unconsciousness. Drinking kava was traditionally a communal activity which involved ceremony. Although kava is still popular in Fiji, Tonga and Samoa, in the Cook Islands the missionaries all but stamped it out. Kava is also a term used for any alcoholic drink, and kava pakari is strong drink.

matu rori

sea cucumbers (also known as bêches-de-mer). Although Rarotonga's lagoon has several species of rori, only two are eaten – the matu rori 'fat rori' and the less popular rori toto 'blood rori'. Matu rori can be eaten raw or cooked, usually with butter, garlic and spices. If you want to eat rori toto, you'll have to cook it first.

potato salad

commonly called mayonnaise, potato salad is a favourite food at every big or special feast

raw fish

no Cook Islands feast would be complete without raw, marinated fish, such as trevally, parrot fish or tuna.

The fish is cut into cubes and soaked in lemon juice or a mixture of vinegar, oil and salt, and is eaten with chopped onion and coconut cream. It may also be served with chopped tomatoes, cucumbers and carrots.

When ordering raw fish, be careful to pronounce the name correctly. Ika, pronounced with a soft 'i' (with almost an 'h' sound before the i) means 'fish', whereas 'ika said with a guttural 'i' (as in 'if') means a woman's genitals.

rukau

a delicacy in which tender, young taro leaves are mashed and mixed with coconut cream, salt and chopped onion

At the Market

I'd like to buy ...	'Inangaro au i te 'oko ...
I'm just looking.	'Akarakara 'ua nei au.
How much does this/that cost?	'E a'a te moni i teia/te ra?
Can you reduce the price?	Ka tika 'i a koe kia tuku i te 'oko ki raro mai?
Where can I buy a ...?	Ka 'aere au ki 'ea 'oko ei i tetai ...?
Where's the nearest store?	Tei 'ea te toa vaitata mai?
How many?	'E 'ia?
How much?	'E 'ia te oko?

GETTING AROUND
Bus

Rarotonga has a bus that goes one way around the island and another that goes the other way. The island has a circumference of only 33km, with high jagged mountain peaks, white sandy beaches and a beautiful blue lagoon that can be seen from the bus wherever it is on the road. The beauty about the bus service is that you can flag one down anywhere along the road.

RAROTONGAN MAORI

WOODCARVING

One of the most widespread traditional artforms in the Cook Islands was woodcarving, in which the gods of the old religion were often depicted. These squat figures, described in general as fisherman's gods or called by the name of the particular god they represent, are similar in appearance to the Tangaroa image that has become the emblem of the Cook Islands.

Souvenirs & Artefacts

adze	axe-like hand tool used for ceremonial purposes, made from a stone blade bound to a carved wooden handle
'akaariari	exhibition
'apinga 'akama'ara	souvenir (lit: thing remember)
'apinga tarai	sculpture (lit: thing chip)
'are	building
ei	necklace
ei kaka	an ei made of flowers, traditionally given to anyone arriving from or going on a journey

ei katu	flower tiara
marae	ancient, open-air family or tribal religious meeting ground, marked by stones
pareu	common clothing worn by men, women and children in the Cook Islands, consisting of a length of fabric wrapped around the body
patu 'akama'ara	monument (lit: wall remember)
pate	carved, wooden slit drums
pupu	tiny shells used to make ei (necklaces)
rito hats	hats woven from fine, bleached pandanus leaves
ta'ito	ancient
tiki	symbolic human figure
titaevae	colourful and intricately sewn applique works, traditionally made as burial shrouds, but also used as bedspreads or cushion covers

Geographical Terms

beach	tapa ta'atai
cave	ana
coral reef (raised)	makatea
country	vao rakau
earth	one/'enua
earthquake	ngaruerue 'enua
farm	pāma
hill	tiketike

RAROTONGAN MAORI

SEASONS

autumn	tuatau pururū'anga rau rakau
spring	tuatau tupu'anga rakau
summer	tuatau vera/kokoti
winter	tuatau anu; mate'anga rakau

DID YOU KNOW ...	A Ra'ui is the traditional method of conservation used in the Cook Islands. During a Ra'ui, nothing can be taken from a ra'ui area, which is designated by traditional leaders.

lake	vai roto
mountain	maunga
mountain range	au tua'ivi
mountain trail	ara maunga
ocean	moana
public toilet	'are meangiti o te katoatoa
reef	akau
river	kauvai
road	mataara
rock	toka
ruins	au ngā'i purupururū
	(lit: places fallen)
sea	moana
seasons	au tuatau
valley	ō
village	'oire/tapere
well	rua vai

FESTIVALS

Christmas and New Year

over the Christmas and New Year period, there are many parties, feasts, family celebrations and all kinds of merry-making involving presents, food and alcohol.

On the island of Aitutaki, a dance team from one of the seven villages visits each of the other villages, spending an hour or so performing traditional dances and inviting the host village to join in. When the drumming is good, many take part. After each dance, people throw money in a large basin, with the best dance team getting the most money. On New Year's Day, another village team does the rounds. This is called koni raoni or 'Round the Island' dancing.

Members of a dance team aren't allowed to drink alcohol during the round – which lasts about eight hours! The more daring ones, however, get a big drinking coconut, pour half the milk out and then fill it up again with whisky, gin or their favourite spirit. This way they can drink the coconut openly. It's only much later in the day that their secret is revealed through their new style of dancing.

Constitution Day

August 4th, the date on which the Cook Islands became self-governing, in free association with New Zealand. On Rarotonga, celebrations including traditional dancing, singing and sports last for about a week.

Nuku pageant

on October 26, Gospel Day (the day on which Christianity arrived in the Cook Islands), members of the three vaka (traditional divisions) of Rarotonga island perform a dramatised account of a biblical story on the lawn of one of the Cook Islands mission grounds

RAROTONGAN MAORI

NAMESAKES

There's no differentiation between male and female names in the Cook Islands, and names are often given to commemorate an event that happened around the time of someone's birth. If big brother had just left the island to go to school on another island when you were born, you might've ended up as 'Schooltrip'. Or if he won a medal at the Commonwealth Games, you could be 'Silver Medal'.

LEGENDS
Tapuae Tai (One Foot Island)

A man and his son were out fishing on the eastern reef of Aitutaki. He was good fisherman as well a warrior. A war had taken place in his village, Tautu, on the main island, and he could see the dark smoke rise up into the sky above the trees. Since he wasn't in the village, the enemy knew he'd be out fishing, and warriors set out to find and kill him.

From the distance they could make out the outline of two people in the lagoon close to the beach of the islet. But when they arrived they discovered only one set of footprints in the sand. They followed the footprints and found the man on the other side of the islet awaiting his end. The enemies killed the man and left his body where it fell.

When they'd gone, the son – who'd been helped up a pandanus tree by his father, who's footprints the father had stepped over as they hurried into the bush – came out of hiding. He covered his father's body with coconut fronds and dragged it along the shallow water inside the reef to the beach. After that, the little islet was called Tapuae ta'i, 'One footprint island'.

How Aitutaki Got Its Highest Mountain

The island of Aitutaki was quite flat, and Rarotongan islanders were always bragging to the Aitutakians about their beautiful mountains. This made the Aitutakians so angry, that one night, after paddling across the ocean to Rarotonga, being careful not to be seen by anyone, they stole ashore on the western side of the island. With their powerful , they dug out the top half of a mountain.

In their haste, the Rarotongans dropped a few huge black rocks at a place now called 'Black Rock'. Back on at Aitutaki, they dropped some black boulders at Nikaupara, Reuren and at Pirikiatu. Once in place, the stolen piece of mountain rose to about 90m above sea level, and was called Mounga Pu, meaning 'mountain trunk'.

TIME & DATES
Days

Monday	Monite
Tuesday	Ru'irua
Wednesday	Ru'itoru
Thursday	Paraparau
Friday	Varaire
Saturday	Ma'anakai
Sunday	Sabati

Months

January	Tiānuare
February	Peperuare
March	Māti
April	'Aperira
May	Me
June	Tiūnu
July	Tiurai
August	'Aukute
September	Tepetema
October	'Okotopa
November	Noema
December	Titema

DID YOU KNOW ... Very few of the old kikau houses, with their pandanus-thatched roofs, remain in the Cook Islands. In the Southern Group islands, only Aitutaki has a traditional-style village, called New Jerusalem. Today in Rarotonga, it's illegal to build and live in the traditional type of house that today's generation of elders grew up in.

RAROTONGAN MAORI

NUMBERS

0	kare
1	ta'i
2	rua
3	toru
4	'ā
5	rima
6	ono
7	'itu
8	varu
9	iva
10	nga'uru
11	nga'uru-ma-ta'i
12	nga'uru-ma-rua

TUMUNU

A tumunu is a get-together involving, beer, singing and music held on the island of Atiu. Tumumus have been held since kava was banned by missionaries. At a tumunu, also known as a bush beer school, drinkers line up in front of a bartender, who ladles beer into a coconut shell cup. The beer is swallowed in a single gulp and returned to the bartender to fill for the next person in line. At some point in the evening, the barmtender calls the gathering to a close by tapping on the side of the tumunu with the empty cup and saying a short prayer.

The locally produced beer drunk at the tumunu, called bush beer, is brewed from oranges, bananas, pawpaws or hops. Visitor to the tumunu should bring around a kilogram of sugar or the equivalent in cash as a donation toward the next brew.

Tumunu is also the term used for the hollowed-out coconut palm stump traditionally used as a container for brewing beer.

RAROTONGAN MAORI

13	nga'uru-ma-toru
14	nga'uru-ma-'ā
15	nga'uru-ma-rima
16	nga'uru-ma-ono
17	nga'uru-ma-'itu
18	nga'uru-ma-varu
19	nga'uru-ma-iva
20	rua nga'uru
21	rua nga'uru-ma-ta'i
22	rua nga'uru-ma-rua
23	rua nga'uru-ma-toru
30	toru nga'uru
39	toru nga'uru-ma-iva
40	'ā nga'uru
50	rima nga'uru
60	ono nga'uru
70	'itu nga'uru
80	varu nga'uru
90	iva nga'uru
100	'anere
101	'anere-ma-ta'i
110	'anere ta'i nga'uru
115	'anere tai nga'uru-ma-rima
120	'anere rua nga'uru
190	'anere iva nga'uru
200	rua 'anere
1000	ta'i tausani
1001	ta'i tausani e ta'i
10,000	nga'uru tausani
100,000	'anere tausani
one million	ta'i mirioni
10 million	nga'uru mirioni
100 million	'anere mirioni
one billion	ta'i pirioni

SAMOAN

SAMOA

INTRODUCTION

The Samoan language is a member of the Samoic language group, which forms a part of the larger Austronesian language subgroup. It is related to Tongan, Tahitian, Hawaiian and other Polynesian languages. While Samoan is not mutually intelligible with other Polynesian languages, you may readily notice the closeness of the basic vocabulary as well as the sounds.

Samoan is spoken as a first language by approximately 250,000 indigenous Polynesians of American Samoa and the independent nation of Samoa. In addition, there are approximately 300,000 Samoans living outside the Samoan islands, principally in New Zealand, the US and Australia, who maintain varying degrees of competency in Samoan. Regional differences in the Samoan language are minimal and would not be noticeable to beginners in the Samoan language.

While Samoan is the first language of the people of Independent Samoa and American Samoa, English is widespread as a second language. Visitors will have no problem using English for basic needs, even in the most rural of villages. However, Samoans take a great deal of pride in their language and culture, and visitors who try to use the Samoan language will find their attempts will be met with respect and appreciation.

Samoan people are very patient and gracious towards visitors. If you should encounter difficulties with the pronunciation of some words or in understanding what's being said, don't be discouraged. It's a sign of respect to the Samoan people that you're using the language, and your efforts will be greatly appreciated. However, have an open mind and don't be put off by the occasional laughter or smiles as you speak Samoan. Humour is prominent in Samoan society, especially verbal humour.

SAMOAN

PRONUNCIATION

Samoan has five vowel sounds, which have both long and short pronunciations, and 13 consonant sounds. The consonants h, k and r were added to the writing system to help 'Samoanise' foreign words.

Vowels

The five vowels are pronounced much the same as in many European languages. Each of these vowels can be lengthened – a long vowel is a prolonged articulation of the vowel sound. For example, the vowel a is pronounced as *ah*, while the vowel ā is pronounced *ahhh*. In the writing system, vowel length is indicated by a macron over the vowel (ā, ē, ī, ō and ū).

PRONOUNS

Samoan distinguishes four different meanings of the pronoun 'we'. The forms for three or more people are tātou and mātou. Tātou includes the listener or listeners, while mātou excludes them. When only two people are referred to (we two), the dual forms, tā'ua and mā'ua, are used. Tā'ua includes the listener, but if the speaker uses mā'ua, it includes the speaker and someone else.

I	a'u/'ou
you	'oe/'e
he/she/it	'o ia
we (dl)	tā'ua/mā'ua
we (pl)	tātou/mātou
you (dl)	'oulua
you (pl)	'outou
they (dl)	lā'ua
they (pl)	lātou

SAMOAN

Short Vowels

a   as the 'a' in 'father'
e   as the 'e' in 'leg'
i   as the 'i' in 'pizza'
o   as the 'o' in 'no'
u   as the 'u' in 'duty'

Long Vowels

ā   as the second 'a' in 'grandma'
ē   as the 'ay' in 'hay'
ī   as the 'ey' in 'key'
ō   as the 'oe' in 'chosen'
ū   as the 'ue' in 'Sue'

Diphthongs

When two vowels occur together, they result in diphthongs or glides. Each vowel in the diphthong is articulated, although the resultant sound is a blend of both sounds.

ai   similar to the 'i' in 'night'
oi   similar to the 'oy' in 'toy'

Consonants

There are 13 consonants in the Samoan alphabet (f, g, h, k, l, m, n, p, r, s, t, v and ʼ). Most of the letters sound more or less like their English equivalents. However, a few are pronounced differently.

g   as the 'ng' in 'sing' (never as in 'good')
p   as the 'p' in 'pot', but without aspiration, or the puff of breath which follows the sound in English
r   as the 'r' in 'rib' (often replaced with 'l')
s   as the 's' in 'sit' (never as the 's' in 'pleasure')
ʼ   the sound made between the words in 'uh-oh'. The glottal stop is indicated by an apostrophe (ʼ).

SAMOAN

Colloquial Pronunciation

Modern Samoan has two styles of pronunciation, often termed the k-style and the more formal t-style. The t-style is the style used in writing, in the media, in education and in religious contexts, and is characterised by the use of t, n and g, as well as k and r in borrowed words. The k-style (or colloquial speech) is the form of spoken Samoan most often used by native speakers when speaking casually or when using the language for traditional Samoan activities. The k-style is characterised by rapid, casual speech and by a pronunciation style that substitutes k for 't', g for 'n', and l for 'r'. Children learn to speak using mostly the k-style of Samoan, but begin to learn the formal t-style upon entering school. Native speakers are able to switch from one style of the language to the other depending upon the situation. The t-style is used when speaking to non-Samoans, so you may find it difficult to practise the k-style since many native speakers feel that the t-style is the appropriate form for a non-Samoan to be using. Below is an example of the two forms. Remember that the k-style, although spoken, is never written.

t-style	Tātou nonofo i'inā.	Let's sit there.
k-style	Kākou gogofo i'igā.	Let's sit there.

Stress

Stress falls on the final syllable of a word if it's a long vowel or a diphthong, otherwise it falls on the second-last syllable.

Written Samoan

In modern written Samoan, the long vowel marker and the glottal stop are seldom used, even in the classroom. Children learning Samoan are expected to be able to know the correct pronunciation of a word from context. Thus, a native speaker would be able to distinguish between the following:

o lona tama	('o lona tamā)	his/her father
o lana tama	('o lana tama)	her child

SAMOAN

MEETING PEOPLE

Samoan people view visitors from other countries as honoured guests who are treated with the same respect and courtesies afforded chiefs and religious people within Samoan culture. A person is often called by the place from which they come (see page 189). A person from the island of Savai'i may be referred to as a Savai'i or 'o le Savai'i.

It's said that the sudden appearance of the first European ship over the horizon in 1722 made it look as though the ship was 'bursting forth' (pā) from the 'heavens' (lagi). Hence the term for 'Europeans', pālagi (also papālagi). Perhaps the most important factor leading to wholesale acceptance of Christianity in the islands of Samoa was a legendary prophecy made by the war goddess Nafanua that a new religion would arrive from the sky and be embraced by the people, bringing peace and prosperity to the land.

Gagana Fa'aaloalo (Respect Language)

The Samoan culture places great emphasis on public display of deference and respect to others. This takes place through both verbal and non-verbal means. Strangers, visitors, the elderly, professionals and titled people are shown honour by a shift in verbal and non-verbal language from the common speech styles used in everyday life to a more elaborate style. This 'respect

---

IFOGA

The most serious crimes require the ranking member of an offender's family to endure the humiliating but face-saving ritual of ifoga, the begging for forgiveness. The guilty person's matai must kneel down, covered with a 'ie tōga (fine mat), before the offended party's house until they're invited to enter. This must be done day after day until the wronged party is satisfied that the offence has been atoned for by the humility of the perpetrator's matai.

SAMOAN

language' has distinct features, such as specialised vocabulary (especially nouns and verbs), special forms of address that refer to an individual's title, job or special status, use of the t-style language when addressing non-Samoans and members of the clergy, more careful articulation and increased volume, and less give-and-take conversation. Changes in body language include a more formal, rigid posture, less direct eye contact and an increase in spatial distance. The language of respect is used only when addressing someone else, never in direct reference to the speaker.

Visitors should be aware that the Gagana Fa'aaloalo is a means to show honour and deference, and is used by Samoans even among friends and family in public situations. However, as a speaker unfamiliar with the language, if you're addressed in a formal style and indicate that you don't understand, speakers will automatically adjust to a more common style to accommodate you. By adjusting to your level, the speaker is also showing respect to the novice.

Gagana Fa'amatai (Chiefly Language)

A visitor to the Samoan Islands cannot help but be impressed with the many elaborate public ceremonies that are used to show honour and respect to important people and visitors. The long and ornate speeches that are given at these ceremonies are crafted by Samoan chiefs and exemplify the special place that language has in Samoan society. The Gagana Fa'amatai, or 'Chiefly Language', is a highly specialised speech style used in all traditional

BODY LANGUAGE

It's perfectly normal in the Samoas for members of the same sex to hold hands and display friendship in public, but open displays of affection between men and women, married or not, will be met with disapproval. Samoan men are required to obtain the approval of a woman's family before publicly showing interest in her.

Samoan ceremonies, including the 'ava (kava ceremony), lagi (funeral), fa'aipoipoga (wedding), saofa'i (title investiture) and numerous other ceremonial exchanges.

Samoan tulāfale (orators) and ali'i (chiefs) spend years perfecting this style, and non-titled people attending the chiefs learn this style only through long years of service. Upon the attaining of a matai (chief) title, a man or woman is expected to be well versed in this style and be able to represent his or her family in an appropriate manner in public.

The Gagana Fa'amatai, in addition to all of the features of the Respect Language, is characterised by the use of proverbs, biblical quotes, references to historical incidents, genealogies and a strict adherence to form. Indeed, a speech, even though well conceived, may not be acceptable to other chiefs if the speaker omits a required section or topic from the anticipated sequence.

Visitors aren't expected to be able to use or understand speeches given in the Gagana Fa'amatai, since its mastery takes years of practice. It's common to have a spokesperson speak on behalf of a non-Samoan visitor on such occasions.

Greetings & Goodbyes

The people of Samoa use a handshake for initial greetings or farewell. The handshake in Samoa is a single pump motion rather than the repeated up and down motion characteristic of Western countries. Kissing on the cheeks as a greeting is common among close friends and family members. It's acceptable to remain seated while shaking hands. It's customary to say tōfā soifua (goodbye) rather than tālofa (hello) when passing by someone in the evening.

Hello. (any time of day)	Tālofa.
Hi.	Mālō.
Goodbye.	Tōfā soifua.
Bye. (inf)	Fā.
How are you?	'O ā mai 'oe?
Fine, thanks.	Manuia lava, fa'afetai.
What's your name? (inf)	'O ai lou igoa?

SAMOAN

What's your name? (pol)	'O ai lou suafa?
My name's ...	'O lo'u igoa 'o ...

I'm leaving.	So'u alu.
See you sometime.	Toe feiloa'i.
Let's go.	Se'i tātou ō.

Etiquette

Perhaps the most important aspect of traditional Samoan life is respect, even veneration, for those perceived to be higher than oneself. Children show respect for their parents, women for their husbands, 'āiga for their matai and tulāfale for the ali'i. Visitors, teachers, doctors, politicians, ministers and priests are also held in great esteem.

Visitors to Samoa can expect that initial encounters will lean more towards formal and respectful forms of communication. As familiarity increases, you'll encounter less formality and more use of common words and phrases as well as body language. Remember that it's always a compliment to the person you're speaking to when you use more formal ways of communicating. It's customary to use the word fa'amolemole 'please' for any request, and fa'afetai 'thank you' after receiving any service or assistance.

Shoes should be removed when entering a fale (house). When invited into a fale, sit cross-legged or cover your legs. Never enter during prayers or meetings, and don't make noise in the area while prayers are being said. If you inadvertently enter a village during sā (nightly vespers), sit down and wait quietly until the all clear is sounded.

Don't eat while walking through a village, and don't pass a meeting of chiefs while carrying a load on your shoulders or with an open umbrella.

If you'd like to swim at a village beach, climb a mountain, take photos or merely have a look around, be sure to ask permission beforehand of someone in the appropriate village.

When passing in front of someone, lower your head and say tulou or 'excuse me'. If someone says tulou to you, reply E lē āfāina, which means 'That's quite all right'.

Sā

Sā, which literally means 'sacred' or 'taboo', is the nightly vespers or devotional and it is taken very seriously in Samoa. Sometime between 6 and 7 pm, or thereabouts, a village gong or large wooden drum sounds, signifying that the village should prepare for sā. All activity comes to an abrupt halt and automobile and foot traffic stops. When the second gong is sounded, sā has begun.

This time is used for devotionals and prayers in individual family homes, and should not be interrupted under any circumstances. Samoan villagers who ignore the regulations of sā incur fines.

When a third gong is sounded, usually after about 15 or 20 minutes, sā is over and activities may be resumed. If you're caught out in a village during sā, stop what you're doing, sit down and quietly wait for the third gong to sound. These rules aren't applied as strictly in Apia or the Pago Pago Harbor area.

'Ava Ceremony

'Ava, or **kava**, the *Piper methysticum* plant, a cousin to the black pepper, is a drink made from the ground root. It's an analgesic, low in calories and serves as a mild tranquilliser, a pain killer, a diuretic, an appetite suppressant and a soporific.

The 'ava ceremony is ritual in Samoa. Every meeting of **matai** and many government gatherings are preceded by an 'ava ceremony. Originally the village **taupou**, a ceremonial virgin who was often the daughter of an **ali'i** (chief), was responsible for mixing the drink, but now it can be mixed by any young woman.

The ground root is mixed with water in a **tānoa** (**kava** bowl). Participants seat themselves in a circle, with the bowl at the back area of the **fale**. When the 'ava is ready, a **tulāfale** calls out the

WHERE ARE YOU GOING?

The question **E te alu 'i fea?** 'Where are you going?' is often rhetorical and may be used as a way of initiating conversation. This question may be asked even if the answer's obvious.

SAMOAN

names of the participants in order of rank. A server scoops the drink into half a coconut shell and presents it to the recipient, who drips a few drops on the ground as an offering to God and says manuia, the Samoan equivalent of 'cheers', before drinking it. Others answer soifua, meaning 'to your health'. Visitors who find the taste objectionable may pour the remainder onto the ground without causing offence.

People

baby	pepe
boy	tama
chief (of family)	matai
family; descent group	'āiga
caucasian	pālagi/papālagi
girl	teine
high chief	ali'i
man	tamāloa
man (untitled)	taule'ale'a
minister	faife'au

old woman (term of respect)	lo'omatua
old man (term of respect)	toea'ina
orator; talking chief	tulāfale
person	tagata
spirit/ghost	aitu
spirit medium	taulāitu
traditional healer	taulāsea
village mayor	pulenu'u
woman	fafine

SAMOAN

Nationalities

I'm (a/an) ...	'O a'u 'o le ...
American Samoan	'Amerika Sāmoa
American	'Amerika
Australian	'Ausetalia
Belgian	Peleseuma
British	Peretānia
Canadian	Kānata

DRESS CODES

Western dress is becoming more common among the younger people of Samoa, but many Samoans and visitors wear a lavalava, a wraparound piece of brightly coloured fabric. On formal occasions, women wear a puletasi, a long skirt worn under a matching tunic.

The Samoan equivalent of the business suit is the 'ie faitaga, an undecorated lavalava of suit-coat material with pockets.

When swimming in rural areas near villages, walking about in a bikini or shorts should be avoided, and a sarong or lavalava should be worn. Men can wear it around the waist, and women around the waist or tied at the neck. Asking a local resident how to wrap a lavalava can be a good conversation starter.

SAMOAN

Chinese	Saina
Danish	Tenemaka
Dutch	Hōlani
Egyptian	'Aikupito
Fijian	Fiti
Filipino	Filipaina
French	Farani
German	Siāmani
Irish	Aialani
Israeli	'Isarā'elu
Italian	ītālia
Japanese	Siapanī/Iāpani
Korean	Kōlea
Mexican	Mesikō
New Zealander	Niu Sila
Russian	Rūsia
Spanish	Sēpānia
Swedish	Suetena
Swiss	Suisilani
Tahitian	Tahiti
Tongan	Toga

FAMILY & SOCIAL STRUCTURE
The Fa'amatai

The fa'amatai (matai system of government) is in effect throughout the Samoan islands, and has its roots in ancient Samoan culture. Each nu'u (village) comprises a group of 'āiga (extended families) which include as many relatives as can be claimed.

The 'āiga is headed by a chief, called a matai, who represents the family on the fono (village council). Matai, who may be male or female, are normally elected by all adult members of the 'āiga.

The matai are responsible for law enforcement and for deciding punishment for infractions that may occur in their village. Social protocol is taken extremely seriously, and crimes such as manslaughter, adultery, violence, insubordination and defiant behaviour are punishable by various penalties, fines, and ultimately, banishment.

The Fono

The fono (village council) consists of the matai of all 'āiga associated with the village. All of the family matai meet once each week at the fono to discuss village issues. A family chief may be either an ali'i (high chief) or a tulāfale (orator). The highest ali'i of the village sits at the head of the fono. In addition, each village has one pulenu'u (a combination of mayor and police chief). The pulenu'u is elected every three years and acts as an intermediary between the village and the national (or territorial, in the case of American Samoa) government. The tulāfale is an orator who liaises between the ali'i and outside entities, carries out ceremonial duties and engages in ritual debates.

The symbols of the tulāfale's office are the fue (fly whisk), which represents wisdom, and the to'oto'o, a staff representing chiefly authority.

Meetings are held in a fale fono, a traditional open house, and all participants in the meetings are seated according to rank, the ali'i at the ends and the orators along the front.

When a high-ranking chief dies, villages effectively close down. The sea around the village is also closed during the period of mourning – no fishing or swimming is permitted.

Other Organisations

Members of a village are divided into several social organisations. The matai belong to the fono (village council). The society of taule'ale'a (men without chiefly titles), known as the 'aumaga, is the strength of the village. Traditionally taule'ale'a were the warriors of the village. The aualuma is the society of females who were born or grew up in the village. They are responsible for providing hospitality and entertaining guests. The wives of matai, mostly women who have married into the village, are called faletua ma tausi. Their role is to provide leadership and direction for the village women.

All women in the village belong to a relatively new organisation called the komiti, which is responsible for the health and sanitation of the village and its members. Since the coming of Christianity, two other organisations, the 'ekālesia (community of village church members), headed by the faife'au (minister), and the 'autalavou (Christian youth organisation) have also been added to the Samoan social structure.

brother (female speaking)	tuagane
child/children	tamaitiiti/tamaiti
child (adopted)	fānau fai
daughter (father speaking)	afafine
daughter (mother speaking)	tamateine
family	'āiga
father	tamā
husband	tāne
mother	tinā
sibling (same sex)	uso
sister (male speaking)	tuafafine
son (father speaking)	atali'i
son (mother speaking)	tamatama
spouse	to'alua
wife	āvā

Staying with a Family

A visitor might experience the 'real' Samoa during a stay in the islands by spending a night or two in a rural village. To do this, you must make friends with a local resident, then an invitation usually won't be far behind. If you're staying with a village family, politely refuse invitations to stay with other families in the same village, since this may bring shame upon your hosts.

It's customary to bring some food as a gift for the family when you arrive. This food gift is called an oso. In place of, or in addition to an oso, you may also want to give a modest monetary gift to the family when you leave. Small gifts representative of your home country – anything that's difficult to obtain in a village – will usually be graciously received. If you've taken photos of the family, they would treasure any copies you may send them later.

FOOD

Eating in Samoa is a social activity in which people tend to eat together and share their food. When dining with others, wait until everyone's been served before starting your meal. A short prayer before eating is also customary. If food is placed before you, it shouldn't be refused. Simply accept graciously and eat as much as you can. Cleaning your plate completely is a sign that you may still be hungry and you may be given more food by your host. The host cannot finish eating before the guests. Always thank your host after you've eaten. Samoans frequently offer a finger bowl in which to wash your hands after the meal.

Restaurants have a full range of cuisine, and prices are generally set by a menu. Tipping isn't customary but is becoming more common. The market is a good place to sample traditional Samoan foods. Visiting a Samoan family will also expose you to a wide range of traditional foods, especially in rural villages. It's easy to meet people in Samoa, and you'll find that invitations to visit families in town or in home villages are common. Hospitality, courtesy, and friendliness are cornerstones of the Samoan culture.

The best sources of local produce and fish (as well as crafts) are the markets in Apia and Pago Pago.

Let's say grace.	Se'i fai le lotu.
Thank you (very much).	Fa'afetai (tele).
You're welcome.	Fa'afetai fo'i.
Has the drinking water been boiled?	'Ua puna muamua le vai inu?
Are you hungry/thirsty?	'Ua 'e fia 'ai/inu?
I'm hungry/thirsty.	'Ua 'ou fia 'ai/inu.
I'm full.	'Ua 'ou mā'ona.
I'm a vegetarian.	'Ou te lē 'ai 'a'ano o manu.
I've already eaten.	'Ua 'uma ona 'ou 'ai.
The food is good.	E mānaia le mea'ai.
That's enough.	'Ua lava.
More, please.	Toe 'aumai, fa'amolemole.

SAMOAN

Local Dishes

fa'alifu talo/fa'i/'ulu

 boiled taro/banana/breadfruit steamed in coconut cream

ota

 raw fish, usually skipjack, yellowfin tuna or other reef fish
 served with coconut cream, salt and lime peelings or lime leaf

palusami

 onion, salt and coconut cream, wrapped in taro leaves and
 then baked

supo ese

 mixture of papaya, sago and coconut cream which may be
 sweetened with sugar. A deliciously refreshing and not-too-
 sweet dish that can be enjoyed at any time of the day.

At the Market

Bargaining isn't customary at the market and with street vendors,
but multiple purchases from a vendor may invite negotiations,
especially if performed with a sense of humour.

DID YOU KNOW ...	Before missionaries arrived, all Samoans had a personal aitu – a fish, bird or other animal that they held as sacred. When they converted to Christianity, they were required to prove the sincerity of their conversions by denouncing their aitu, which missionaries regarded as symbols of paganism. Aitu still have prominence in Samoan culture, but these days the word frequently refers to any mischievous or wandering spirit.

How much is the ...?	E fia le tau o le ...?
How much each?	E ta'i fia?
How much is all of this?	E fia le tau aofa'i?
Where can I buy a ...?	'O fea e fa'atau ai se ...?
I want a ...	'Ou te mana'o 'i se ...
Do you have any ...?	'O maua ni ...?
Do you have any more?	E iai ni isi?
I don't want that/this.	'Ou te lē mana'o 'i le mea lenā/lea.
Can I have it at a cheaper price?	E mafai ona 'e fa'apa'ū la'itiiti i lalo?
I'm just looking.	Se'i o'u matamata.

GETTING AROUND

Samoa is a small country, so business can be facilitated through the use of local customs and practices. Always remember that the use of polite forms of speech shows respect for the person you're talking to.

The Fale

The traditional Samoan-style house is called a fale. The word can also refer to any kind of house or building, including western-style houses, called fale pālagi.

The traditional Samoan fale is a rounded structure without walls. The thatched sugar cane leaf (lau tolo) roof is supported by wooden posts and the floor consists of a rock foundation topped with coral rock or pebbles, which is then covered with woven coconut leaf and pandanas mats. Blinds made of woven coconut leaves are lowered to keep out wind and rain. There's often a smaller kitchen fale near the main home used for meal preparation.

Traditional fales are still found throughout Independent Samoa, though many are now constructed with concrete slab floors and tin roofs. Western-style square fale with walls, windows and doors are becoming more common.

SAMOAN

Every village has one prominently located fale, the fale fono, in which the village council meets. Hibiscus, frangipani and ginger flowers are sometimes used to decorate the building and surrounding grounds, and coconut fronds may be plaited around all the posts in preparation for special occasions.

Geographical Terms

beach	matāfaga
blow hole	pupū
bridge	ala laupapa
cloud	ao
coconut tree	niu
coral	'amu
dirt/earth	'ele'ele
environment	si'osi'omaga
forest	vao matua
grass	mutia
house	fale
island	motu
lagoon	aloalo/taitafola
lake	vaitūloto
lava	lava
moon	māsina
mountain	mauga
natural pool	loto

QUESTION WORDS

What?	'O le ā?
When (past/future)?	'O anafea/āfea?
Who?	'O ai?
How many?	E fia?
Where to/from?	I/mai fea?
Which?	'O lēfea?
Why?	'Aiseā?

TABOO LANGUAGE

Samoan custom discourages the public use of words referring to sex, genitals and bodily functions such as urination and defecation. This especially applies between relatives of the opposite sex. The sacred bond between brother and sister, feagaiga, requires family members to always be careful of what is said in the home and in public. Swearing exists in Samoan as in other languages, but it should be avoided by the novice.

ocean	vasa
passage through reef	ava
river	vaitafe
sand	oneone
sea	sami
seaweed	limu
sky	lagi
spring	vaipuna
star	fetū
sun	lā
tree	lā'au
village green	malae
waterfall	āfu
wharf	uafu

Animals

ant	loi
bat	pe'a
bird	manulele
cat	pusi
chicken	moa
dog	maile
dove	lupe
eel (fresh water)	tuna

SAMOAN

eel (ocean)	pusi sami
fish	i'a
gecko	mo'o
hermit crab	uga
horse	solofanua
mouse	'isumu
pig	pua'a
shark	malie
skink/lizard	pili
turtle	laumei

Plants

breadfruit tree	'ulu
cocoa	koko
coconut (brown)	popo
coconut (green)	niu
flower	fugālā'au
fruit	fuālā'au
hibiscus	'aute
lime	tīpolo
orange	moli
pandanas	laufala
papaya	esi
tree	lā'au

NAMES

Traditionally, Samoan family members call each other
by their given names rather than by familial roles such
as 'mother' or 'father'. A child may be named in honour
of a friend, relative or ancestor, or to commemorate a
recent occurrence such as Christmas or a hurricane. A
child may also be given a name taken from the Bible,
or from either Samoan or world history.

Souvenirs & Artefacts

fala

two very desirable household mats woven from the pandanas leaf are the fala papa (floor mat), which is a thick and coarsely woven mat, and the fala lili'i or fala moe (sleeping mat) which is finely woven with a fringe of colourful yarn

siapo

the bark cloth known as siapo, or tapa, made from the inner bark of the paper mulberry tree (u'a), provides a medium for some of the loveliest artwork in the Samoas. Originally used as clothing and coverings, siapo is still used in customary exchanges.

'ie tōga

fine mats woven from specially prepared pandanus leaves, which look and feel like fine linen or silk. Along with other woven mats and siapo, they make up 'the gifts of the women' that must be exchanged at many formal Samoan ceremonies. Agricultural products comprise 'the gifts of the men'.

SAMOAN

TRADITIONAL CURES

Samoa is rich in traditional medicine and folklore. Traditional cures include medicines and poultices made from plants and hands-on interaction between the healer and the patient.

There are several types of Samoan healers — the fa'atosaga (midwives), those who practise fofō (massage), the fofōgau (orthopaedists capable of setting broken bones), the taulāsea (herbalists who draw on the Samoan rainforest in their treatment of disease) and the taulāitu or spirit healers who banish troublesome aitu (spirits).

A typical taulāsea is able to diagnose and treat over 200 different diseases, many of which have no Western equivalent, with a combination of 120 or more rainforest plants.

SAMOAN

'ato	basket
'ie faitaga	men's undecorated formal lavalava (sarong)
'ie lavalava	sarong
'ie tōga	finely woven mat made from pandanus fibres
ili	traditional coconut leaf braided fan
mama	ring
paopao	traditional ourigger canoe
puletasi	long skirt and tunic worn by Samoan women
pūlou	hat
siapo	tapa cloth
tānoa palu 'ava	kava bowl
taulima	bracelet
'ula	necklace

THE PE'A

The pe'a (Samoan tattoo) is a centuries-old tradition that identifies the tattooed person as a proud and courageous Samoan. Although many young men have opted not to undergo this painful procedure, growing numbers, especially in Independent Samoa, are now choosing to be tattooed, possibly as a mark of Samoan identity.

Tattoos normally cover a man's body from the waist to the knees. Sometimes women also elect to be tattooed, but their designs cover only the thighs. Women's tattoos are never shown in public except on community occasions, such as when performing the siva or 'Samoan dance'.

A man receiving a tattoo lies on the floor while the tufuga (tatoo artist) works through the painful process of tapping the design into the skin with an instrument made from boar tusk and turtle shell. The man being tattooed must not be left alone in case aitu, or spirits, cause him to become ill. In most cases, the entire procedure takes a month to complete.

FESTIVALS & HOLIDAYS

Aso o le Fu'a (Flag Day)
> on April 17 cultural and sporting events are held in American Samoa to mark the raising of the American flag on this day in 1900

Aso o le Palolo (Palolo Day)
> traditional day in both Samoa and American Samoa for gathering the delicious palolo 'reef-worm'. The palolo rises from the coral reefs to mate in October or November each year, on the seventh day after the full moon, before sunrise for just a few hours. The blue-green worms are a prized delicacy in much of the South Pacific, and are said to taste like creamy caviar. Parties and musical festivities take place on the beaches throughout Samoa in the build up to their appearance. When the worms finally surface at around midnight, crowds carrying nets and lanterns wade into the sea to scoop them up.

'O le Teuila (Teuila Festival)
> held in Samoa in the first week of September, the Teuila Festival features a wide range of cultural and sporting events

T„to'atasi (Independence Day)
> celebrated June 1–3 to commemorate the independence of the former Western Samoa in 1962. Activities include a range of cultural and sporting events.

Aso Sā Pa'epa'e; Lotu a Tamaiti (White Sunday)
> celebrated in both American and Independent Samoa on the second Sunday in October, White Sunday is a religious and social holiday established by the early missionaries to honour children

Music

Traditional Samoan songs are written to tell stories, commemorate events or praise notable individuals. Love songs are popular, as are patriotic songs extolling the virtues of the Samoas.

SAMOAN

Dancing & Fiafia

fiafia

refers to a lavish presentation of Samoan dancing and singing performed at large Samoan gatherings. They are frequently presented now at the larger hotels, usually accompanied by a huge buffet dinner. The dancing is performed by groups accompanied by guitars, ukelele and the beating of traditional wooden gongs or rolled mats.

koneseti

koneseti (concert) is a village play or musical presentation in which participants dress in a variety of costumes and accept money or other donations based on the quality of the performance

---

SAMOAN LITERATURE

Albert Wendt is Independent Samoa's most renowned scholar and author. His novels, *Leaves of the Banyan Tree*, *Flying Fox in a Freedom Tree*, *Pouliuli*, *Birth and Death of the Miracle Man*, *Inside Us the Dead*, *Shaman of Visions* and *Sons for the Return Home*, all look at the issue of maintaining the values of fa'a Samoa (traditional Samoa) and its social structures.

Samoan performance poet and writer Sia Figiel uses traditional storytelling forms in her work. Her first novel, *Where We Once Belonged*, tells the story of a young woman searching for her identity in a traditional Samoan village. Figiel has also published a volume of short stories called *The Girl in the Moon Circle*.

The novel *Alms for Oblivion* by Fata Sano Malifa follows the wanderings of Niko in his tireless search for self-justification.

sāsā
> traditional group action dance featuring synchronised motions and clapping performed to the rapid beat of a wooden gong or hollow tin

siva
> the traditional Samoan dance performed by women or men with hand and feet motions that are unique to Samoa

siva afi (fire knife dance)
> today the dance, usually performed as a grand finale, is the dramatic favourite of most visitors. Dancers gyrate, leap and spin while twirling nifo 'oti (flaming knives) in time to the rapid beat of a wooden gong or a hollow tin.

taualuga
> traditionally, the final dance of the evening. (The taualuga is also the word for the finishing touch on the roof of a fale.) The taualuga was usually a siva danced by the taupou (ceremonial virgin), who performed dressed in traditional attire such as a fine mat or tapa cloth.

LEGENDS
Creation Legend

Before there existed any sea, earth, sky, plants or people, the god Tagaloa lived in the expanse of empty space. He created a rock, commanding it to split into clay, coral, cliffs and stones. As the rock broke apart, the earth, sea and sky came into being. From a bit of the rock came a spring of fresh water.

Next, Tagaloa created man and woman, whom he named Fatu and 'Ele'ele ('heart' and 'earth'). He sent them to the region of fresh water with a command that they people that area. He ordered the sky, which was called Tu'ite'elagi, to prop itself up above the earth, and using starch and teve, a bitter root plant and the only vegetation available at this early date, he made a post for it to rest upon.

SAMOAN

Tagaloa then created Pō and Ao ('night' and 'day'), who in turn bore the 'eyes of the sky', the sun and the moon. At the same time Tagaloa made the nine regions of heaven, which he filled with all sorts of gods.

In the meantime, Fatu and 'Ele'ele were busy peopling the area where they'd been sent. Tagaloa, reckoning that all these earthlings needed some form of government, sent Manu'a, another son of Pō and Ao, to be the chief of the people. From that time on, the tupu (king) was called Tu'i Manu'a tele ma Samoa atoa, which means 'King of Manu'a and all of Samoa'.

Next, the lands were divided into islands or groups of islands so the world consisted of Manu'a, Fiji, Tonga and Savai'i. Tagaloa went to Manu'a, apparently noticing a void between it and Savai'i, and up popped Upolu and then Tutuila. The final command of Tagaloa before he returned to the expanse was 'Always respect Manu'a – anyone who fails to do so will be overtaken by catastrophe, but men are free to do as they please in their own lands'. Thus, Manu'a became the spiritual centre of the Samoan islands and, to some extent, of all Polynesia.

Myth of the Coconut

Though there are countless versions of the origin of the coconut tree, this is one of the most romantic. The beautiful young woman Sina, who lived on Upolu, kept a pet eel called Tuna, who was the incarnation of Tui Fiti, the king of Fiji. When he grew to be as long as a man, Sina released him into the pool where she bathed every day. When Tuna tried to court Sina she became frightened and ran away, but Tuna soon followed. Sina finally begged a gathering of chiefs in a nearby village to kill Tuna. Hearing of the plan to kill him, Tuna pleaded with Sina that she plant his head next to her house. He said, 'From me a tree will grow that will provide for your every need. You will have food, water and shelter always. And every time you drink from my fruit, you'll be kissing me'. Feeling pity for Tuna, Sina did as she was asked. Next time you drink from a coconut, you'll notice Tuna's tiny face looking up at you.

Gateway to the Underworld

The Falealupo Peninsula figures prominently in local legend. Samoans believe the gateway to the underworld of the aitu (spirits) is found at the place where the sun sets in the sea.

According to tradition, there are two entrances to the underworld at Falealupo at a place known as the Fafā, one for chiefs and another for commoners. During the night, these spirits wander abroad, but at daybreak they must return to the underworld.

TIME & DATES

Saturday is considered market day in Samoa, when people make their purchases for the large communal meal that's prepared for Sunday. Sunday is considered a day of church attendance and rest. Most rural villages don't encourage recreational activities such as swimming on Sunday.

Days

Monday	Aso Gafua
Tuesday	Aso Lua
Wednesday	Aso Lulu
Thursday	Aso Tofi
Friday	Aso Faraile
Saturday	Aso To'ona'i
Sunday	Aso Sā

Months

January	Ianuari
February	Fepuari
March	Mati
April	'Aperila
May	Mē
June	Iuni
July	Iulai
August	'Aokuso/'Aukuso
September	Sētema
October	'Oketopa
November	Nōvema
December	Tēsema

SAMOAN

SAMOAN

Time

last week	le vaiaso 'ua te'a
day before yesterday	le aso tala atu ananafi
yesterday	ananafi
last night	anapō
earlier today	analeilā
today	le asō
now	nei
soon/almost	toeitiiti
later today	nānei
tomorrow	taeao
day after tomorrow	le aso tala atu taeao
this week	le vaiaso nei
next week	le vaiaso 'ā sau
1999	afe iva selau iva sefulu iva
morning	le taeao
afternoon	aoauli
evening	afiafi
night	pō
midnight	vaeluaga o le pō

NUMBERS

0	o
1	tasi
2	lua
3	tolu
4	fā
5	lima
6	ono
7	fitu
8	valu
9	iva
10	sefulu
11	sefulu tasi
12	sefulu lua

SAMOAN

13	sefulu tolu
14	sefulu fā
15	sefulu lima
16	sefulu ono
17	sefulu fitu
18	sefulu valu
19	sefulu iva
20	lua sefulu
21	lua sefulu tasi
30	tolu sefulu
40	fā sefulu
50	lima sefulu
60	ono sefulu
70	fitu sefulu
80	valu sefulu
90	iva sefulu
100	selau

SAMOAN CURRENCY

Samoa has its own currency, the tālā, which is based on the decimal system. The paper currency and coins exhibit scenes or objects from Samoa, and all feature the portrait of the Head of State, His Highness Malietoa Tanumafili II.

one cent	sene
two cents	lua sene
five cents	lima sene
10 cents	sefulu sene
20 cents	lua sefulu sene
50 cents	lima sefulu sene
two dollars	lua tālā
five dollars	lima tālā
10 dollars	sefulu tālā
20 dollars	lua sefulu tālā

SAMOAN

101	selau ma le tasi
110	selau sefulu
111	selau sefulu tasi
200	lua selau
300	tolu selau
1000	afe
2000	lua afe
10,000	sefulu afe
100,000	selau afe
1,000,000	miliona

When counting people, the prefix to'a- is added to the number. Thus 'three books' is e tolu tusi while 'three people' is e to'atolu tagata.

The word for 'first' is muamua. To get other ordinal numbers, add lona before the number – for example, lona lua 'second', lona lima 'fifth'.

TAHITIAN

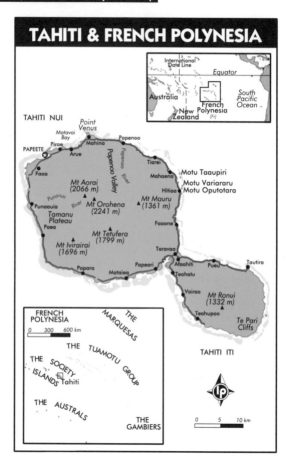

TAHITI & FRENCH POLYNESIA

International
Date Line

Equator

Australia

French
Polynesia
(Fr)

New
Zealand

South
Pacific
Ocean

TAHITI NUI

Point
Venus

Matavai
Bay

Mahina

Papenoo

PAPEETE

Pirae

Arue

Tiarei

Faaa

Papenoo Valley

Mahaena

Motu Taaupiri

Mt Aorai
(2066 m)

Hitiaa

Motu Variararu
Motu Oputotara

Punaruu
River

Mt Orohena
(2241 m)

Mt Mauru
(1361 m)

Punaauia

Tamanu
Plateau

Faaone

Paea

Mt Tetufera
(1799 m)

Mt Ivirairai
(1696 m)

Taravao

Papara

Mataiea

Papeari

Afaahiti

Pueu

Tautira

Teohatu

Vairao

Mt Ronui
(1332 m)

**FRENCH
POLYNESIA**

0   300   600 km

THE
MARQUESAS

Teahupoo

Te Pari
Cliffs

THE TUAMOTU GROUP

TAHITI ITI

THE
SOCIETY
ISLANDS   Tahiti

THE AUSTRALS

THE
GAMBIERS

0   5   10 km

TAHITIAN

INTRODUCTION

Tahitian (Reo Mā'ohi) is a Polynesian language spoken throughout French Polynesia (also known as the Society Islands). There are 150,000 indigenous inhabitants of this vast archipelago of 130 islands in the central Pacific.

French Polynesia consists of five major island groups, scattered over an area as large as Europe. The Society Islands, of which Tahiti is the hub, are the main group. Among these, the best known are Moorea, Raiatea and Borabora. To the north and east of the Society Islands are situated the low-lying Tuamotu archipelago (also known as Paumotu). To the north of the Tuamotus lie the spectacular volcanic Marquesas group, some 1200 kilometres from Papeete. To the south of Tahiti lies the Austral group (Rimatara, Rurutu, Tupuai, Raivavae and Rapa), and to the south-east the Gambier archipelago (Mangareva).

The languages of these major groups correspond to five distinct languages – Marquesan (spoken in two major dialects, north-west (Nuku Hiva) and south-east (Hiva Oa); Tuamotuan (with a multitude of dialects); Tahitian (with minor dialectal differences throughout the Society Islands); Mangarevan (the language of the Gambier archipelago); and Rapan and the dialects of the Austral Islands.

The Tahitian language is pre-eminent in French Polynesia, for a number of reasons. The island of Tahiti, the largest and most populous island, was where the first missionaries settled in 1797 at Point Venus in Matavai Bay. With the conversion of King Pomare to Christianity in 1815, it became the language of evangelisation. Missionaries soon published elementary books in Tahitian, then religious texts, and finally the complete Bible, *Te Parau a te Atua*. As Tahitian pastors converted the islanders to Christianity, written Tahitian gained currency over the other dialects and languages of the Society Islands. This dominance has been accentuated even further through Tahitian-language newspapers, newsletters and political tracts, and more recently by its extensive use in radio and in television, which reaches even the most remote islands via satellite transmission.

Today, a Tahitian Academy, Te Fare Vanaa, created in 1972, the Tahitian equivalent of the Académie française, generates modern Tahitian equivalents of Western technological terms.

PRONUNCIATION

Tahitian isn't particularly difficult for English speakers to pronounce, as most Tahitian sounds are also found in English. Likewise, the Tahitian alphabet, devised in the 19th century, is fairly simple to use.

Vowels

As with all other Polynesian languages, Tahitian has five vowels, pronounced much as they are in Italian or Spanish.

a   as the 'a' in 'father'
e   a sound falling between the 'e' in 'bet' and the 'ay' in 'bay'
i   as the 'ee' in 'see'
o   as the 'o' in 'more'
u   as the 'oo' in 'zoo'

Tahitian and most other Pacific languages have a second series of vowels, the same as those we have just seen, only pronounced twice as long. You can get an idea of this lengthening by comparing the pronunciation of English 'icy' and 'I see', both distinguished in sound only by the length of the final vowel.

The missionary devised spelling of Tahitian doesn't distinguish vowel length, since the missionaries felt that native speakers naturally knew whether a given word had short or long vowels. However, for non-Polynesians the long vowel is indispensable, since vowel length can change the meaning of a word. Long vowels are indicated by a macron over the vowel (ā, ē, ī, ō and ū).

parau	to speak	api	full
pârau	pearl-shell	'āpī	new

Diphthongs

When two vowels appear together, they retain their original pronunciation. Thus ai sounds like the 'y' in 'my', ei like the 'ay' in 'hay', au like the 'ow' in 'vow' and ou like the 'oe' in 'toe'.

Consonants

The consonants are pronounced much as they are in English, with a few modifications.

h   as the 'h' in 'house';
when preceded by 'i' and followed by 'o', as the 'sh' in 'shoe' (as in iho 'only/just')

p   as the 'p' in 'sponge', not as the 'p' in 'path' (not followed by a puff of breath)

r   often rolled like in Scottish English or Spanish

t   as in the 't' in 'stand', not as the 't' in 'talk' (not followed by a puff of breath)

'   glottal stop. This sound occurs between two vowels and is like the sound you hear between the words in 'uh-oh'. In Tahitian, this sound isn't indicated in normal spelling (with a few minor exceptions), since native speakers know where they occur. Foreigners, however, aren't so lucky – the glottal stop is indicated by the apostrophe ( ) in this chapter.

Stress

In Tahitian, if the final vowel of a word is a long vowel, it is stressed. If not, the second-last vowel is stressed.

WORD ORDER

The basic word order in Tahitian is Verb–Subject–Object.

ENGLISH INFLUENCE ON TAHITIAN

English had a major influence on the Tahitian language in the 19th century, due to the presence of English-speaking missionaries, as well as whalers and sailors who frequented the waters of the Society Islands. There are many English loanwords in Tahitian, although when a word was borrowed it took on a Tahitian flavour. Borrowed words must conform to Tahitian pronunciation – Tahitian has fewer consonants than English, no two consonants occur together, and every word ends in a vowel.

Therefore, when a word with English 'b' was borrowed into the language, the 'b' became 'p', as in purūmu 'broom', since there's no 'b' in Tahitian. The sound changes between English and Tahitian can be summarised as follows:

English	Tahitian	English	Tahitian
b	p	broom/road	purūmu
k/g	t	gallon	tārani
s/z/sh	t	razor	reta
l	r	flour/bread	faraoa

One of the most interesting loanwords in Tahitian is purūmu, from English 'broom'. This word has also come to mean 'road' in Tahitian. The reason for this meaning shift is quite unexpected. One of the first roads to be built in Tahiti was called 'Broom Road' (later known as 'Rue de Rivoli'), which encompassed the entire island. A punishment for people convicted of minor offences was to sweep the road with a broom, and so it is that the Tahitian word for 'road', purūmu, is derived from the English word 'broom'.

TAHITIAN & THE MODERN WORLD

Although Tahitian borrowed a number of terms from English, it was not content to simply adopt terms for things that were new or unknown to Tahitian culture. Tahitians drew upon their own rich language to derive terms for modern technology. Some are very colourful and expressive.

accelerator	ha'a-pūai-ra'a-pereo'o (lit: make-power-ra'a-vehicle)
aeroplane	manu-reva (lit: bird-space)
airport	tahua-manu-reva (lit: field-bird-space)
ambulance	pereo'o-ma'i (lit: vehicle-sick)
bank	fare-moni (lit: house-money)
bar	fare-inu-ra'a (lit: house-drink-ra'a)
battery	'ōfa'i-mōrī-pata (lit: stone-light-switch on)
bedroom	piha-ta'oto (lit: room-sleep)
bicycle	pereo'o-tāta'ahi (lit: vehicle-pedal)
bra	tāpe'a-tītī (lit: hold-breast)
camera	pata-hoho'a (lit: click-image)
can-opener	pātia-punu (lit: stab-container)
car	pereo'o-uira (lit: vehicle-lightning)
cathedral	fare-pure-ra'a-rahi (lit: house-pray-ra'a-big)
chair	pārahi-ra'a (lit: sit-ra'a)

TAHITIAN

Note that in Tahitian, the nominative marker ra'a is
used to indicate that the word is the subject of a verb.

---

cheese	pata-pa'ari (lit: butter-hard)
dentist	taote-niho (lit: doctor-tooth)
drawer	'āfata-'ume (lit: box-pull)
fork	pātia-mā'a (lit: spear-food)
glasses	titi'a-mata (lit: filter-eye)
goat	pua'a-niho (lit: pig-tooth)
horse	pua'a-horo-fenua (lit: pig-run-ground)
hose	uaua-pipi-tiare (lit: rubber-water-flower)
hospital	fare-ma'i (lit: house-sick)
lavatory	fate-iti (lit: house-small)
motorcycle	pereo'o-tāta'ahi-uira (lit: vehicle-pedal-lightning)
office	piha-pāpa'i-ra'a-parau (lit: room-write-ra'a-word)
post office	fare-rata (lit: house-letter)
refrigerator	'āfata-fa'a-to'eto'e-ra'a (lit: box-make-cold-ra'a)
submarine	pahī-hopu-moana (lit: ship-dive-ocean)
telephone	niuniu-paraparau (lit: wire-speak)
television	'āfata-teata-na'ina'i (lit: box-cimema-small)

TAHITIAN

MEETING PEOPLE

Before the arrival of missionaries, Tahiti and surrounding islands had a highly stratified society. The paramount ari'i rahi (chief) ruled over a wide area. He was supported by lesser chiefs (ari'i ri'i), who were hereditary chiefs of an extended group. There were also the to'ofa who ruled over a district (mata'eina'a) or village (nu'u). In addition, there were also the ra'atira or hereditary land owners descended from a younger branch of the ari'i, and of lower social standing the common people (manahune) and slaves (teuteu). People of non-Polynesian descent are called popa'ā, and tourists te mau rātere

TAHITIAN

Hello; Good morning.	Ia ora na, nana.
Goodbye.	Pārahi, nana.
Welcome.	Maeva, mānava.
Excuse me; Sorry.	E'e, aue ho'i e.
Thank you.	Māuruuru roa.
Good luck!	Fa'aitoito!
Cheers!	Manuia!

QUESTION WORDS

What?	Eaha?
Who?	O vai?
Where?	Tei hea?
Where to?	I hea?
Where from?	Nō hea mai?
When? (future)	Afea? āhea?
When? (past)	Ināfea? ī anāfea?
How?	Nāfea?
How much?; How many?	E hia moni?
How many (people)?	To'ohia?
Why?	Eaha ... ai?

TAHITIAN

FOOD

Food and eating are major preoccupations in Tahiti, where traditional Polynesian dishes and modern Polynesian adaptations of Western (mā'a popa'ā) and Oriental dishes vie with one another in tempting the palate.

Traditional Tahitian Dishes

Mā'a Tahiti, as traditional Tahitian dishes are known, is based on fresh produce. Mā'a Tahiti is traditionally eaten with the fingers.

i'a ota

raw fish salad, or Tahitian salad. This dish, in which the fish is marinated in fresh lime juice and served in coconut milk, appears on most Tahitian menus. The abundance of fresh fish makes this dish a favourite among fish-lovers.

fāfaru

fish fermented in sea-water. This dish, highly prized by Polynesians, may surprise the visitor with its pungent odour – it's the Tahitian answer to smelly French cheeses.

LOCAL FISH	
bonito	'auhopu
dorado/dolphin-fish	mahimahi
fish	i'a
flying-fish	mārara
manta ray	fāfā piti
raw fish	i'a ota
red mullet	'i'ihi
salted fish	i'a rapa'au
tuna	'a'ahi
shark	ma'o
stingray	fai
turtle	honu

'īpō
> boiled bread made from flour and coconut juice, with a rather heavy consistency. Grated coconut and sugar are sometimes added.

mai'a
> bananas. This fruit comes in many varieties, and is eaten cooked or raw. Perhaps the most interesting banana dish, almost a banana salami, is pīere (sun-dried banana), which keeps almost indefinitely.

pua'a fanau'a
> roast suckling pig. One of the Polynesian favourites, this dish is cooked on red-hot stones and covered with leaves in a hīmā'a (earth oven).

po'e
> pounded or crushed fruit (most commonly banana or papaya) mixed with pia (arrowroot starch) and flavoured with a vānira (vanilla pod). The mixture is then wrapped in banana leaves and cooked in a ground oven, after which it's sprinkled liberally with coconut milk.

pōpoi
> paste made from banana, breadfruit or taro

Other favourite Tahitian dishes are 'uru (roasted breadfruit), fē'ī (mountain bananas or plantains, which are always eaten cooked), mahi (fermented breadfruit), 'uhi or 'ufi (yam), taro (taro) and 'umara (sweet potato).

Sauces

Some delicious local sauces you're bound to encounter include:

miti ha'ari
> coconut-milk sauce

miti hue
> coconut fermented in a hue (gourd) filled with water and prawn heads

taioro
> made from grated coconut, salt water and fresh-water prawns

At the Market

The Papeete market, Te Mātete in the centre of the downtown area is a colourful, bustling place which has a wide variety of produce and a large selection of local arts and crafts.

How much is that ...?	Ehia moni terā ...?
I'd like ...	E hina'aro vau ...
Show me ...	A fa'a'ite mai 'oe ...
I'll take ...	E rave au ...
How many?	Ehia?
That's expensive.	Mea moni rahi.
Thank you very much.	Māuruuru roa.

GETTING AROUND
Geographical Terms

bay	'o'o'a
beach	pae tahatai
city	'oire
coral	pu'a/to'a
country	fenua
district	mata'eina'a
flower	tiare
islet	motu
land	fenua
moon	'āva'e
mountain	mou'a
lagoon	pae moana; tairoto
ocean	moana
promontory	'ōtu'e
reef	a'au
reef edge	pae a'au
river	anavai
sand	one
sea	miti
star	feti'a
stone	'ofa'i

sun	mahana
town	'oire
valley	fa'a
waterfall	topara'a pape
wave	'aremiti
wind	mata'i

Souvenirs & Artefacts

monoi
coconut oil blended with the fragrance of the tiare flower,
widely used to add fragrance to toiletries

pandanus
pandanus leaves are woven to make hats, bags and mats.
Some of the finest pandanus work comes from Rurutu in
the Austral Islands.

petroglyphs
designs carved into stone, featuring representations of
octopuses, tortoises, canoes, the sun, human forms and
geometric shapes.

tapa
material produced by beating tree bark until it's paper thin,
and then decorating it. Tapa was once used to make pareus
(sarongs) and tiputa (poncho-like garments). Today, it's
produced for ceremonial use and for collectors, particularly
in the Marquesas.

TAHITIAN

DEMONSTRATIVES

'this' (near the speaker in space and time)	teie
'that' (near the person addressed in space and time)	tēnā
'that' (not near the speaker in space and time)	terā

tīfaifai

appliquéd or patchwork blankets produced on a number of islands. Introduced by missionaries, the craft now has a number of important uses. People are wrapped in a tīfaifai as a sign of welcome. They're considered important wedding gifts, and may also be draped over a coffin.

ti'i

statues carved from blocks of basalt or volcanic tuff, or from wood. Generally erected on or near a marae, ti'i are believed to have had a religious and symbolic function, representing deified ancestors or a protective power. They also were carved in bas-relief and on weapons, paddles, canoes and utensils.

wood carving

ceremonial canoe paddles and prows and intricately carved handles for fly-switches and fans are displayed in museums, and sometimes still produced

basket (coconut, oval)	'ara'iri
basket (pandanus)	'ete
basket (coconut)	'ō'ini
basket (general)	pāniē
fan	tāhiri
hat	tāupo'o
mat (coconut)	pāua
mat (pandanus)	pe'ue
patchwork quilt	tīfaifai
pearl	poe
sarong (paréo)	pareu

VERY LONG

The word roa, 'long', is also used to mean 'very'.

very short	poto roa
very beautiful	purotu roa

FESTIVALS

Fa'ahe'e

this major surfing competition takes place at Punaauia beach every year in September

Hawaiki Nui Canoe Race

the major sporting event of the year, a 116km race held in November. On the first day, contestants race from Huahine to Ra'iatea, continuing on to Taha'a on the second, then on to Bora Bora on the final day. The event grips the country and almost brings it to a standstill, as canoe teams from all over the Society Islands and Hawaii compete in this prestigious sporting event.

canoe	va'a
outrigger	ama
paddle	hoe
race	horora'a

Te Heiva; Te Ta'urua Tiurai

the major festival of the year is the Tiurai, or Heiva i Tahiti. Spanning four weeks, it begins in late June and reaches a high point on 14 July, Bastille Day. Celebrations include dancing competitions, and sporting events such as canoe races, javelin throwing, stone-lifting contests and fruit-carrying races.

drum with membrane	pahu
wooden hand-held drum	tō'ere
Western-type drum	tariparau
singing (traditional or modern)	hīmene

Te Heiva no te Pahu Nui o Taha'a

during this event, canoes spread out across the lagoon and herd fish into an enclosure by beating the water with stones. This 'Stone Fishing Festival' takes place in Taha'a during the last week of October. Activities include singing, dancing and craft displays, and a fire-walking ceremony which precedes the festival.

TAHITIAN

TAHITIAN

bottom fishing	tautai tāoraora
line fishing	tautai hī
net fishing	tautai 'upe'a
throw-net fishing	tautai 'upe'a tāora
torch fishing	tautai rama
underwater fishing	tautai hopu

MUSIC & DANCE

WELCOME SONG: MAEVA

Maeva Maeva e
　Welcome, Welcome

Maeva Maeva e
　Welcome, Welcome

E! tera mai te hei
　Here is the necklace

Tiare tiare Tahiti
　of tiare Tahiti (gardenia)

Maeva i Tahiti
　Welcome to Tahiti

Maeva e
　Welcome

Maeva te mau hoa
　Welcome, friends

Maeva e
　Welcome

E! tera mai te hei tiare e
　Here is the necklace of flowers

Tiare tiare Tahiti
　Flowers, tiare Tahiti

Tahitian Dance

One tradition that can be seen practically every day of the year is the world-famous 'ori tahiti (Tahitian dancing), the best known of which is the tāmūrē

te 'ori	Tahitian dance, especially the tāmūrē
te 'aparima	dance accompanied by hand gestures
te hivinau	couples dance around the orchestra
te pā'ō'ā	dance accompanied by singing and thigh-slapping
te 'ōte'a	dancers are arranged in rows
te tāmūrē	girating dance in which couples dance close together

TAHITIAN

LEGENDS

There were many gods in the traditional Polynesian pantheon, who are widely known in myth and legend around the Pacific islands to this day. The islands of Ra'iatea and Taha'a – which once had greater prominence than Tahiti – are associated with many of the earliest myths and legends of the Society Islands.

Ra'iatea was believed to have been settled directly from Samoa, and was given the name Hawaiki in memory of the homeland (Savaii). Taha'a was at that time named Kuporu or Uporu, after Savaii's sister island Upolu. Tahiti has assumed a

TAHITIAN

THE MARAE

One of the major centres of community activity was the traditional temple or marae, built of stone or coral blocks. The key element of the marae was the ahu, an upper platform or altar, set up for offerings to the gods. This was the most sacred place, where the high priest (tahu'a nui) put the effigies of the gods (ti'i) and the spirits of the ancestors (to'o), which he removed from wooden tabernacles (fare atua). Behind the ahu stood wooden objects symbolising birds and messengers of the gods. In front of the ahu were monolithic stones representing the ancestors. In the middle of the marae were fata, altars on which offerings were placed. Only the priests, their servants and the most important chiefs were allowed to approach the fata. Other symbolic objects were arranged around the tahua, or central area, such as pahu (sacred drums), hoe (ceremonial paddles) and tira (ceremonial masts). Each ari'i (high chief) was associated with a particular marae.

The most impressive and best preserved marae on Tahiti today is the Marae Arahurahu, near Pa'ea on the west coast of Tahiti. Two other important marae are the Marae Mahaiatea near Papara and the Marae Tataa near the Orofero River.

pre-eminent position only in the past two centuries with the ascendancy of the Pomare dynasty, the last of whom, Pomare V, died in 1891.

The first king of Raiatea was the legendary Hiro. He is said to have built the great canoes which sailed as far as New Zealand. The supreme god (atua), worshipped by pre-Christian Tahitians, was called Ta'aroa (Tangaroa in other parts of Polynesia).

TAHITIAN

TIME & DATES
Days
Monday	Monirē
Tuesday	Mahana Piti
Wednesday	Mahana Toru
Thursday	Mahana Maha
Friday	Farairē; Mahana Pae
Saturday	Mahana Mā'a
Sunday	Tāpati

Months
January	Tenuare
February	Fepuare
March	Māti
April	Eperēra
May	Mē
June	Tiunu
July	Tiurai
August	Atete
September	Tetepa
October	Atopa
November	Novema
December	Titema

TAHITIAN

TELLING THE TIME

In Tahitian, time-telling is more specific than in many other Pacific languages.

What's the time?   Eaha te hora?
It's two o'clock.   E hora piti.

Minutes to the hour are expressed by toe, meaning 'remaining'.

It's two minutes to two.   E piti miniti toe e hora piti ai.
It's seven minutes to five. E hitu miniti toe e hora pae ai.

Minutes past the hour are expressed by ma'iri, meaning 'elapse'.

It's ten minutes past two. E hora piti ma'iri hō'ē 'ahuru miniti.
It's two minutes past five. E hora pae ma'iri e piti miniti.

NUMBERS
Cardinal Numbers

1	hō'ē/tahi
2	piti
3	toru
4	maha
5	pae
6	ono
7	hitu
8	va'u
9	iva
10	hō'ē 'ahuru
11	hō'ē 'ahuru ma hō'ē
12	hō'ē 'ahuru ma piti
13	hō'ē 'ahuru ma toru

14	hō'ē 'ahuru ma maha
15	hō'ē 'ahuru ma pae
16	hō'ē 'ahuru ma ono
17	hō'ē 'ahuru ma hitu
18	hō'ē 'ahuru ma va'u
19	hō'ē 'ahuru ma iva
20	piti 'ahuru
21	piti 'ahuru ma hō'ē
30	toru 'ahuru
40	maha 'ahuru

TAHITIAN

PRONOUNS

Tahitian pronouns distinguish three numbers, singular, dual (for two people) and plural (more than two people). In addition, there are two words for 'we' and 'us'. If the person you're talking to is included, the 'inclusive' form is used – if not, then the 'exclusive' form is used.

I	au/vau
you (sg)	'oe
he/she/it	'oia/'ōna
we (dl inc)	tāua
we (dl exc)	māua
you (dl)	'ōrua
they (dl)	rāua
we (pl inc)	tātou
we (pl exc)	mātou
you (pl)	'outou
they (pl)	rātou

There are two forms for 'I' – au and vau. Au is used after words ending in -i or -e, while vau is used elsewhere. There are also two forms for 'he/she' – 'oia and 'ōna. The second form is commonly used to refer to 'he/she' when they've already been mentioned.

TAHITIAN

50	pae 'ahuru
60	ono 'ahuru
70	hitu 'ahuru
80	va'u 'ahuru
90	iva 'ahuru
100	hō'ē hānere
101	hō'ē hānere ma hō'ē
500	pae hānere
1000	hō'ē tauatini
5000	pae tauatini
10000	hō'ē 'ahuru tauatini
100,000	hō'ē hānere tauatini
1,000,000	hō'ē mirioni

PLACENAMES

Pape'ete means 'basket of fresh-water', while the splendid island of Mo'ore'a means 'yellow gecko', a common emblem around the island.

Ordinal Numbers

These are formed by putting a or te before the number, except for tahi (first), which must take a.

first	a tahi; matamua
second	a/te piti
third	a/te toru
fourth	a/te maha
fifth	a/te pae

TONGAN

TONGA

Niuafo'ou

Tafahi

THE NIUAS

Niuatoputapu

International
Date Line
Equator

Australia
Tonga
South
Pacific
Ocean

New
Zealand

SOUTH
PACIFIC
OCEAN

Fonualei
Toku

VAVA'U
GROUP

'Utungake
Vava'u
Neiafu
Late
Pangaimotu

0   50   100 km

Late'iki
(Metis Shoal)

Kao
Lofanga
Ha'ano
Tofua
Panga
Foa
Ha'afeva
Lifuka
HA'APAI
GROUP
Nomuka
'Uiha

Fonuafo'ou
Kelefesia
Hunga
Tonga
Hunga
Ha'apai

NUKU'ALOFA

'Eue'iki

Tongatapu
'Eua
TONGATAPU
GROUP

'Ata

INTRODUCTION

Tongan is a Polynesian language spoken by the people of the Kingdom of Tonga. There are approximately 100,000 people in Tonga, of which about 98% are ethnic Tongans. There are also sizeable communities of Tongans overseas – particularly in New Zealand, though also in Australia and the US.

Tongan is (along with English) the official language of Tonga and is the language most often used in everyday communication. There are three registers or levels of speech in Tongan. Most of the distinctions are to do with verbs, though a number of common nouns are also affected. The common everyday speech is much like informal English – though it's also used in formal situations when referring to (as opposed to speaking to) a person of relatively low rank. The second variety might be referred to as honorific. It is used to refer to someone of status or when speaking directly to someone (anyone) in a formal context. The third register is used only when talking to or about a reigning monarch or deity.

PRONUNCIATION

Being a language whose writing system has only recently been developed, Tongan words tend to be pronounced much as they are written. Thus each letter represents almost exactly the same sound wherever it occurs.

Consonants are always followed by a vowel. In written Tongan, the apparent exception to this rule is the 'cluster' ng. This is pronounced as the 'ng' in 'sing' (not as in 'finger'), so despite being written as two letters, it's actually a single sound.

Vowels

There are five vowels in Tongan and each may be pronounced as long or short. The meaning of words often depends on this distinction, so it's an important feature to get the hang of.

Long vowels are indicated in writing by a macron, or dash, above the vowel (ā). They're pronounced like the short vowels, but are about twice as long, and can change the meaning of a word. For example, that the word pepe means 'butterfly' while pēpē means 'baby'.

The short vowels are pronounced as follows.

a   as the 'u' in 'butter', but slightly longer
e   as the 'a' in 'ham'
i   as the 'ee' in 'meet' (but a bit shorter)
o   as the 'o' in 'wrong'
u   as the 'oo' in 'pool'

Consonants

Most of the 12 consonants in Tongan are pronounced much like their English equivalents. The only ones likely to cause difficulty to an English speaker are ng and the glottal stop ('). The consonant ng is mainly difficult because in English this sound doesn't occur at the beginning of words – which it frequently does in Tongan. The glottal stop isn't considered a letter at all in English but is important in Tongan. It represents the catch in the throat between the words in 'uh-oh'. As with long vowels, the meaning of a word is often changed by the presence or absence of this sound.

| fao | to stretch | faʻo | a nail |
| anga | behavior | ʻanga | shark |

DID YOU KNOW ... Originally, the word vaka referred to 'boat'. When aeroplanes were first introduced to Tonga, a new word, vakapuna, was coined. It's common practice though to use vaka as a generic term for both planes and boats.

TONGAN

Stress

Apart from the macron indicating the long vowel, the only other new speech mark you'll come across in Tongan is ('), which is printed after the vowel as a´, e´, i´, o´ and u´. This indicates stress. In Tongan, words are usually stressed on the second-last syllable, which isn't marked. When, however, the word is to receive special emphasis in the sentence, the stress is shifted to the final syllable – which is what the above symbol indicates.

MEETING PEOPLE
Greetings

The standard greeting when you meet someone is Mālō e lelei, to which the greeting is repeated in reply. Mālō e lelei is literally an expression of pleasure at the good health of the person addressed. Other greetings, and their literal translations, include:

I'm glad we've ...	Mālō e tau ...
made it this far	lava
reached this morning	lava ki he pongipongi´ ni
reached this day	lava ki he 'aho´ ni
got this day	ma'u 'a e 'aho´ ni

When greeting someone you haven't seen for a long time, the greeting Male e mo'ui, 'I'm glad you're living' may be used.

TONGAN LITERATURE

Tales of the Tikongs and *Kisses in the Nederends*, both by the Tongan author 'Epeli Hau'ofa, tell the story of the coming of age of a small Pacific island kingdom called 'Tiko', which is largely based on Tonga.

Other Tongan authors include Konai Helu-Thaman, who has written several anthologies of poems and short stories about Tonga and the decline of Tongan culture, and who co-authored collections of Tongan legends written in both Tongan and English.

TONGAN

Goodbyes

The following are informal expressions used in bidding farewell.

When you're leaving:

Goodbye.	Nofo ā.
Goodbye. (to two people)	Mo nofo ā.
Goodbye. (to three or more people)	Mou nofo ā.

When someone else is leaving:

Goodbye.	'Alu ā.
Goodbye. (to two people)	Mo ō ā.
Goodbye. (to three or more people)	Mou ō ā.

In more formal contexts, the terms 'alu and ō may be substituted with faka'au when you're bidding farewell to someone who's leaving:

MEETING ROYALTY

To show their respect when meeting with royalty and nobility, Tongans wear ta'ovala (woven mats) tied around the waist with coconut sennit. To be without one would be the social equivalent of a European presenting himself to the president or prime minister without a jacket and tie.

When a member of royalty is standing or sitting, Tongans physically lower themselves in relation to him or her as a demonstration of subservience. This may mean approaching on all fours in order to keep one's head lower than the royalty in question.

It's taboo to imitate the actions of a member of royalty in any way. At any gathering at which royalty is present, everyone must take their seats before the guests of honour arrive. Once royalty has been seated, no one else may be admitted (in this instance, Western-style punctuality is vital).

TONGAN

| Goodbye. (to two people) | Mo faka'au ā. |
| Goodbye. (to three or more people) | Mou faka'au ā. |

The appropriate response to both farewells is 'Iō

In Tonga, it's quite common for someone passing you in the street to ask where you're going, Ko ho 'alu 'ena ki fē?, or simply 'Alu ki fē?. You're not expected to give a detailed response – the person's usually just being friendly. The following are common expressions used to respond to this query:

| I'm just coming here. (used when the destination is close by, and often accompanied by pointing to the destination) | (Ko 'eku pehē mai pē) ki heni. |
| I'm going to the shop/town | Ko 'eku 'alu ki falekoloa/kolo. |

Forms of Address
When addressing someone in an informal context – regardless of their rank – it's customary to use the person's first name. Even children address their parents by their first names in Tonga. In indirect reference, a title may be substituted. In formal situations, you would address a person, especially one of rank, by their title.

Titles
boy	tamasi'i
cabinet minister	Minisitā
deacon	tīkoni
gentleman	tangata'eiki
girl	ta'ahine
noble	Nōpele
pastor	faifekau
woman	fine'eiki

Relationship Terms
Own Generation

spouse	mali
same sex sibling (any age)	tokoua
same sex sibling (older than speaker)	ta'okete
same sex sibling (younger than speaker)	tehina
self	kita
brother (female speaking)	tuonga'ane
sister (male speaking)	tuofefine

Parents' Generation

father; father's brother	tamai
father's sister	mehekitanga
mother; mother's sister	fa'ē
mother's brother	fa'ē tangata; tu'asina

Younger Generation

brother's child (female speaking)	fakafotu
daughter	'ofefine
grandchild	mokopuna
sister's child (male speaking)	'ilamutu
son	foha

Older Generation

grandparent	kui (can be used for any ancestor from grandparent upwards)

Just as a person's mother is referred to with the same term as their mother's sister, and their father with the same term their father's brother, so the children of their mother's sister or father's brother (cousins, in English) are referred to by the same terms as their own brothers and sisters. Likewise, a man will refer to his brother's children using the same terms as for his own, and a woman will do the same with her sister's children.

TONGAN

People

matapule	talking chief involved in burial rituals and ceremonies of the nobility
papālangi	foreigner
tevolo	devil spirit
Tu'i Tonga	royal title given to a Tongan ruler
'ulumotu'a	head of extended family
vahenga	high-ranking dancer

Body Language

When approaching someone of high rank, it's polite to keep your head lower than theirs. As an extension of this, it's also polite when you enter a home or office to sit down immediately without waiting for an invitation, before saying why you have come. When passing someone who's seated, you should say tulou, which is equivalent to 'excuse me'.

TONGAN

Social Etiquette

There are a number of other rules that Tongans follow in social contact which may be unfamiliar to visitors.

- Avoid sitting close to a member of the opposite sex whenever possible. When you get into a car which someone else is driving, you should only sit in the front seat if you're of the same sex as the driver. This rule doesn't, of course, extend to your spouse.
- Eat everything you are given. If you can't eat something for medical reasons – say you suffer from diabetes for instance – then it's OK to say so. Otherwise eat up or your host will be offended.
- If someone visits you around morning or afternoon-tea time, don't offer them a hot drink, just serve it. To ask if your guest would like a drink is to imply that you're hoping they won't.
- If you're invited to stay in someone's home as a guest, don't offer payment for your board unless it is asked for. To do otherwise might well insult your host as they'd feel they were being treated like a motel. The same rule applies if someone offers you a ride in their vehicle.
- When approaching the house of someone you know reasonably well, it's customary to call out to the person you've come to visit before you arrive at the door.
- If you are given a gift, you should always try to give one in return.
- Always sit down when you eat. Eating while standing up is considered to be bad manners.

'REAL' RELATIONS

Tongans don't consider relations by marriage to be 'real' relations. For instance, where in English we might speak of our 'aunt and uncle', Tongans would say their 'aunt and her husband'.

- Except for very formal events – such as a church service, or a function where a member of the royal family is to be present – do not arrive on time.

  If the event is scheduled to begin at 7 pm, that doesn't mean that you arrive at 7 pm; it means that you start to think about getting ready at around 7 o'clock – the event will probably get underway at about 8.00 or 8.30 pm.

Letter Writing

Letters in Tongan are usually begun with one of the following:

Dear Sir/Madam   Si'i Tangata'eiki/Fine'eiki

Unlike English business letters which state their business in the first paragraph, Tongans wait until the second paragraph before bringing up the purpose of writing. The first paragraph says how happy you are to write the letter, and hopes the recipient is well and that his or her spouse has gotten over their bout of influenza. After these pleasantries, you're free to proceed with business.

When writing to someone of a high social rank, it's polite to refer to him or her in impersonal terms. Thus, instead of using the pronoun koe, 'you', the writer would use feitu'u' na (lit: your place or position).

The closing will, most often, be one of the following:

Love ...   'Ofa atu ...

Respectfully yours,   Faka'apa'apa atu,

FAKA TONGA

Faka tonga means 'the Tongan way', which encompasses the customs and cultural practices, social rules and rituals of the Tongan people.

FOOD

The traditional method of cooking is known as 'umu (earth oven). 'Umu is much like the Hawaiian 'luau' and the Maori 'hangi'. It's an underground oven where rocks are first heated on an open fire until they're red-hot, then placed at the bottom of a hole. Root crops and portions of meat are then wrapped in banana leaves and placed on the stones. The food is then covered with sacking, which is, in turn, covered with earth to fill the hole. Further banana leaves are placed on top, and the dish is left to roast for about three hours.

These days, most people only use an 'umu to prepare a Sunday lunch or a special feast. At other times food is prepared by more modern methods such as boiling (haka), baking (ta'o), spit roasting (tunu) or frying (fakapaku).

A Tongan meal consists of two main components – root vegetables, which are sometimes referred to simply as me'akai, meaning 'food' (including taro, tapioca, yam, potato, sweet potato, and also breadfruit), and animal products, which are often called kiki (including meat, poultry and fish). The term vesitapolo is used to refer to other vegetables not covered by me'akai (carrots, cabbage, pepper) as distinct from fruits, which are called fua. Breadfruit is not classed as a fruit because it can't be eaten raw. Vesitapolo may appear in dishes mixed with meat but aren't normally served separately.

Local Dishes

faikakai
  pudding made from bread or other starchy foods. Faikakai topai is a pudding made from baked breadfruit, coconut cream and sugar. Yam or taro can be used in place of breadfruit.

'otai
  drink made from fruit pulp, sugar and water

'ota ika
  raw fish marinated in a mixture of lemon juice and salt, then mixed with coconut cream, lemon juice and finely chopped onion, carrot, cucumber and tomato

lū

a dish usually prepared in the 'umu, consisting of meat mixed with taro leaves, coconut cream, onion and salt, and then wrapped in banana leaves (which are discarded after cooking) and baked. Some common varieties of lū are:

lū pulu	lū with corned beef filling
lū sipi	lū with mutton filling
lū pulu masima	lū with salted beef filling
lū ika	lū with fish filling

faikakai	breadfruit pudding
feke	octopus
fingota	shellfish
kumala	sweet potato
'ika	fish
lu pulu	corned beef and boiled taro in coconut cream
lu and talo	taro leaves and roots
manioke	cassava
polas	stretchers of coconut frond on which food is carried and served
'ufi	yams

If a person comes to visit during a meal, it's customary to extend the invitation Ha'u 'o kai, 'Come and eat'. If you want to politely refuse the invitation, say Mālō pē, 'Thanks anyway'. Your host may say Kai ke ke mākona, 'Eat up, have plenty' (lit: eat until you're full). At the end of the meal you might like to thank your hosts with Mālō e fei me'atokoni, 'Thanks for the meal'.

GETTING AROUND
Placenames
Tonga Island

The biggest island in Tonga, and probably your first stop, is known popularly as Tongatapu. Properly, the name is just Tonga (the kingdom is named after the island). The honorific tapu (lit: sacred) is added to its name by virtue of the fact that the king (who was traditionally believed to be descended from the creator god, Tangaloa) lives on it and has his seat of government on it.

Niutoua

In the north-east of Tonga, at the very end of the bus route, lies the proud old village of Niutōua, the capital and seat of government for the first kings of Tonga many years ago. Although the village itself is old, its current name only dates back to the 1950s during the reign of Queen Salote.

The old name of the village was Ha'amene'uli (ha'a = tribe or clan, mene = posterior, 'uli = dirty). According to folklore, in the days when this town was the capital of Tonga, there was once a king who was afraid, almost to the point of paranoia, that someone might try to kill him. Because of this fear, he ordered that anyone wishing to approach him must seat themself on the ground some distance away from him and shuffle forward while remaining seated. Although this practice was not continued after that king died, the people of Tonga never forgot it and so they began to call the people who lived there and tended the royal family Ha'a Mene'uli and later, after the capital was shifted, the village also became known by that name.

PRAY FOR SUNDAY

Public transport isn't available on Sundays in Tonga – if you really need a taxi, you'll need to make arrangements on Saturday. All shops are closed on Sundays, and while you can sit on the beach, swimming isn't generally permitted.

TONGAN

When Queen Salote became the monarch, however, she decided that the name was not appropriate for a town in a nation considered to be Christian, so she renamed it Niutōua (niu = coconut tree, tō = planted, ua = two) after a famous landmark which used to stand at the centre of the royal compound there – two coconut trees planted so close together that they joined together at the base to look like a single tree with a double trunk.

TAKEN FOR A RIDE

To stop a bus or taxi, put your arm out in front of it as it approaches. Taxis in Tonga are generally only distinguished by their number plate, which begins with a 'T'. There are no fare-metres, so it's best to ask someone what the fare for a particular journey should be before getting in – or you might be taken for a ride.

Geographical Terms

beach	matātahi
blow holes (found at Houma)	pupu'a
cave	'ana
hill/rise	hake
island	motu
royal burial tombs	langi
volcano	mo'ungaafi

Souvenirs & Artefacts

kiekie	decorative waist band with dangling strips of pandanus, strands of seeds, bits of cloth of fibre cords
fala fihu	silk-fine pandanus mats
fala tu'i	pandanus mat of double thickness, one layer woven of coarse tofua and the other of fine paongo (both types of pandanus)

TONGAN

popao	outrigger canoe
ta'ovala	waist mat often worn at formal occasions
tupenu	wraparound skirt which extends to just below the knees (for mens) or ankles (for either sex)
kalia	large seafaring canoes

FESTIVALS

The major annual national festival in Tonga is called Heilala Week. This event is held in the week including July 4th – this being King Taufa'ahau Tupou IV's birthday. In recent years, the celebrations have begun one or even two weeks beforehand. Celebrations include music contests, marching, parades and a beauty pageant at which the winner is crowned 'Miss Heilala'. Tupakapakanava, the torch-lighting ceremony in which the northern coastline of Tongatapu is lit up by people carrying flaming torches, coincides with the Heilala Festival.

Some terms and phrases often heard at festivals and feasts include:

fiefia	happy/joyous
kātoanga	feast
lakalaka	group dance, performed standing
ma'alali	celebrate
tau'olunga	solo female dance
mā'ulu'ulu	group dance, performed seated

Tongan speeches always begin by paying respects to everyone in the audience, starting with the most distinguished and progressing down the ranks until everyone has been mentioned either by name or category (such as clergy, ladies and gentlemen). It's polite to refer to 'the king's presence' rather than 'the king' – this is true of any dignitary.

| My respects to the presence of the king. | Tapu mo e 'afio 'a e tama tu'i'. |

I extend my humble regards to you.
(A common ending to a speech.
The honorific term 'eiki may be
added if the audience includes
high ranking dignitaries such as
royalty or nobility.)

Tu'a ('eiki) 'ofa atu.

Any festivity a visitor attends during Heilala Week will probably
feature members of the royal family, and therefore will begin and
end with the national anthem. This is sung at any function
attended by royalty in Tonga.

NATIONAL ANTHEM

'E 'Otua Mafimafi
   Almighty God
Ko homau 'eiki´ koe
   You are our lord
Ko koe ko e falala'anga
   You are the reliable One
Mo e 'ofa ki Tonga
   And you love Tonga
'Afio hifo 'emau lotu
   Look down upon the prayer
'A ia 'oku mau fai ni
   Which we are rendering
'O ke tali homau loto
   And give us our desire
'O malu'i 'a Tupou
   And protect Tupou

DANCE

fire dance

dance in which one or two dancers gyrate, leap and spin while juggling flaming knives to the time of a rapid drumbeat

kailao

the kailao (war dance) is reminiscent of the days when Tongan men set out in canoes to raid neighbouring islands. The rapid movements re-enact violent attacks and are accompanied by loud drumming, fierce cries, stamping feet and the pounding of pate, spear-like poles which represent war clubs.

lakalaka

the most common traditional dance performed in Tonga. Dancers, usually both men and women, stand in rows dressed in costumes decorated with leaves, shells, flowers and pandanus. They sway, sing and tell stories with movements of their hands.

maʻuluʻulu

a dance for which the dancers actually remain seated throughout the performance, using only their hands to convey the story. Hand movements, known as haka, are choreographed by a punake (a respected artist) who also composes the song which accompanies the maʻuluʻulu. This type of dance is often performed at feasts, on holidays and at state functions.

FAKAPALE

Fakapale (lit: to award a prize) is a custom associated with Tongan dance. Originally, dancers received prizes of fine mats and tapa (bark cloth), given in appreciation of their ability. These days they receive money, and the notes are plastered onto their oiled bodies during a performance.

TONGAN

tauʻolunga
  a solo dance which is always performed by a woman. The
  dancer wears a flowing knee-length dress with bare shoulders
  and with flowers in her hair and on her wrists and ankles. A
  man, known as the tulāfale, often dances behind her, making
  no effort to keep in time. It's thought that his bad rhythm
  makes the woman seem all the more talented by comparison.
  The tauʻolunga is performed at village and government
  functions, and women often perform it at their own wedding.

MYTHS & LEGENDS
Munimatamahae & Pungalotohoa

Munimatamahae grew up on the island of Lofanga in Haʻapai.
As a child he was always helpful and obedient to his parents. By
the time he was a young man, he was very strong and hard-
working. The people of the island and his parents were amazed at
the things he did. Work that usually needed a lot of people and
took a long time, Munimatamahae did alone in a very short time.

One day he found out that the couple who looked after him
were not his real parents. They told him his real parents lived on
Tongatapu, so he decided to go and look for them.

He set sail from Lofanga on a kalia (ancient Tongan canoe) and
arrived a few days later at the western end of Tongatapu. He
anchored his kalia and waded the short distance to the sandy beach
of Kolovai. He knew his parents lived near this place so he called
out his father's name as he searched in the thick undergrowth on
the beach. Suddenly he heard his father's faint voice from among
the creepers.

Munimatamahae called again, 'Motuku Veʻevalu, where are you?'.

'I'm here, hiding under these creepers', came the faint reply.

'Why are you hiding and speaking so softly?', inquired
Munimatamahae loudly.

'Stop shouting. All the people here are terrified of
Pungalotohoa, a warrior from Hahake. If he comes around here
he'll break your bones, so don't make such a noise', Motuku
Veʻevalu said.

'Get out from your hiding place', ordered Munimatamahae, 'I'll go and find this man Pungalotohoa. By the way', he explained, 'My name is Munimatamahae, I'm your son. I was washed ashore on the island of Lofanga. A very kind couple brought me up. It was they who told me where to find you'.

At last Munimatamahae was on his way to Hahake. He called at Pungalotohoa's home but found only the servants there. They told him that Pungalotohoa was out fishing. As he was about to leave, Munimatamahae noticed a huge kava plant with lots of bats on it. He took hold of it and uprooted it causing the bats to fly into the air. One of the bats was white and was Pungalotohoa's pet.

As soon as Pungalotohoa saw the white bat in the sky he suspected that something had happened at his home. He returned quickly to learn from his servants that Munimatamahae had been there. He followed Munimatamahae, who was now on his way back to Kolovai carrying the kava plant, and caught up with him at Holonga.

Munimatamahae saw Pungalotohoa coming so he split the kava plant. He shook off the soil on both sides of the road and threw the plant away. The place where he shook the soil off is still marked by two mounds known as Tūtū'angakava (which means 'The place were the kava plant was shaken').

The two great fighters wrestled furiously on the road. The struggle went on for hours. Munimatamahae hurled Pungalotohoa repeatedly to the ground. The blows made him dizzy. Finally he struggled to his feet crying for mercy. He declared that Munimatamahae was the greatest warrior on land, whereas he, Pungalotohoa, was the greatest at sea.

The Ava Fish of Nomuka

There is an island called Nomuka in Ha'apai. Once upon a time there was an old couple called Nifi and Nafa who lived on Nomuka. They had two children – a son, Nomu and a daughter, Iki. The parents named a nearby island Nomukeiki after their children. Nomu and Iki had some special fish, known as 'ava, which they kept in the lake at Nomuka.

At this time, the great god Tafakula was at Kao. He heard that a god from Pasiki in Fiji had come to steal the 'ava fish, so he sent Ha'elefeke, another god, to guard them.

One dark night, the Fijian arrived at Nomueiki. He met Ha'elefeke on the island. Ha'elefeke felt sorry for the Fijian god because he had come such a long way. 'There are plenty of fish in the lake', he thought, 'Why not give him a few?'.

So Ha'elefeke said to the Fijian god, 'Wait until tonight so that Tafakula doesn't see, and I will give you some fish. If I give you them during the day, he might see it and take them off you.'

That night, Ha'elefeke gave the Fijian god a parcel containing two 'ava fish and the god returned happily to Fiji. When he got near Pasiki, though, another god saw him and wanted to know what was in the parcel. He threw a big stone at him which hit the parcel and the fish fell into the sea. They increased in number and today their are many 'ava fish at Pasiki.

TIME
Tongans divide the day into the following sections:

midnight (11 pm until 2 am)	tu'apo
early morning (2 am until dawn)	hengihengi
morning (dawn until 11 am)	pongipongi
noon (11 am until 2 pm)	ho'ata
afternoon and evening (2 pm until 11 pm)	efiafi

Telling the Time
One fact that must be kept in mind when telling the time is that where English speakers refer to the time as half past the hour (half past three, half past four) Tongans refer to the same times by referring to the approaching hour. Thus 3.30 is haafe 'a e faa' (lit: half of four) and 4.30 is Haafe 'a e nima' (lit: half of five).

NUMBERS

The Tongan language has several numbering systems. The system used depends on what is to be counted. For most items, the standard system can be used, but if you want to count certain culturally significant items such as coconuts, yams or fish, you'll need to learn the appropriate terms. Only the standard system will be given here. For the visitor who's interested in the other systems, they are outlined in C. Churchward's *Tongan Grammar* (see page 291).

Standard Counting System

0	noa
1	taha
2	ua
3	tolu
4	fā
5	nima
6	ono
7	fitu
8	valu
9	hiva
10	hongofulu
11	taha-taha
12	taha-ua
20	ua-noa
30	tolu-noa
100	teau
101	teau mā taha

OTHER LANGUAGES

PITCAIRN & NORFOLK ISLANDS

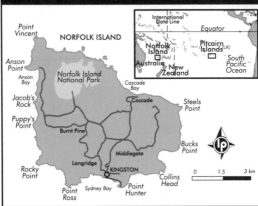

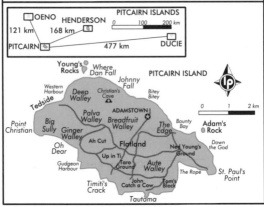

OTHER LANGUAGES

FIJIAN HINDI

Fijian Hindi (sometimes called Fijian Hindustani) is the language of Fijian Indians. It has features of the many regional dialects of Hindi spoken by the Indian indentured labourers who were brought to Fiji from 1879 to 1916. (Some people call Fijian Hindi 'Bhojpuri', but this is the name of just one of the many dialects that contributed to the language.) Most of the vocabulary of Fijian Hindi comes from the eastern Hindi dialects of India, but there are many words from Fijian, especially for names of local flora and fauna (such as dalo 'taro' and walu 'kingfish'). Many words from English are also found in Fijian Hindi (such as room, towel, book and reef).

Fijian Hindi is used in all informal settings, such as in the family and among friends. But the 'Standard Hindi' of India is considered appropriate for formal contexts, such as in public speaking, radio broadcasting and writing. Most of the Hindu majority write in Standard Hindi, using the Devanagari script with a large number of words taken from the ancient language of Sanskrit. Most Muslims use the Perso-Arabic script and words taken from Persian and Arabic. (This literary style is often considered a separate language, called Urdu.) Fijian Indians learn Standard Hindi or Urdu in school along with English, so while they all speak Fijian Hindi informally, not everyone knows the formal varieties.

Some people say that Fijian Hindi is just a 'broken' or 'corrupted' version of Standard Hindi, which they think is the 'pure' or 'correct' language. But the truth is that Fijian Hindi is a legitimate dialect with its own grammatical rules and vocabulary unique to Fiji.

History

Most Fijian Indians are descendants of indentured labourers. Initially most of the Indians sent to Fiji came from the states of Bengal (Bangladesh), Bihar and Uttar Pradesh in north-eastern India. Later, large groups of southern Indians arrived. The great diversity of their languages, religions, customs and subcultures has merged to a certain extent over the years.

Other Indians, largely Punjabis (mostly Sikhs from north of Delhi) and Gujeratis (from the north of Bombay), voluntarily came to Fiji soon after the end of the indenture system. Both groups are now a kind of business elite in Fiji.

Pronunciation

Fijian Hindi is normally written only in guides for foreigners, and transcribed using the Roman alphabet. Since there at least 42 different sounds in Fijian Hindi and only 26 letters, some adjustments have to be made.

Vowels

a	as the 'a' in 'about' or 'sofa'
ā	as the 'a' in 'father'
e	as the 'e' in 'bet'
i	as the 'i' in 'police'
o	as the 'o' in 'obey'
u	as the 'u' in 'rule'

Diphthongs

ai	as the 'ai' in 'hail'
āi	as the 'ai' in 'aisle'
au	as the 'o' in 'own'
oi	as the 'oi' in 'boil'

Fijian Hindi also has nasalised vowels, as in French words such as *bon* and *sans*. This is shown with a tilde ( ) over the vowel or with the letter 'n' if there's a following consonant.

PRONOUNS	
I/me	ham
you (pol)	āp
you (inf)	tum
we/us	ham log

Consonants

The consonants b, f, g (as in 'go'), h, j, k, l, m, n, p, s, v, y, w, and z are similar to those of English. The symbol č is used for the 'ch' sound as in 'chip' and š is used for the 'sh' sound as in 'ship'.

Fijian Hindi has two 't' sounds and two 'd' sounds – all different from English. In 't' and 'd' in English, the tip of the tongue touches the ridge above the upper teeth, but in Fijian Hindi, it either touches the back of the front teeth (dental) or is curled back to touch the roof of the mouth (retroflex). The dental consonants are shown as t and d and the retroflex ones as ṭ and ḍ, and they're important in distinguishing meaning.

ātā	coming	āṭā	flour
tab	then	ṭab	tub'
dāl	dahl (lentils)	ḍāl	branch

HINDU SYMBOLIC RITES

A Hindu temple symbolises the body, in which the soul resides. Union with God is achieved through prayer and by ridding the body of impurities. Meat cannot be eaten before entering a temple and shoes must be removed, as leather, coming from sacred cattle, is considered impure.

Fire and water are used for blessings. Water carried in a pot with flowers is symbolic of the Mother. Burning camphor symbolises the light of knowledge and understanding. When illuminated, the soul merges with the Great Soul. The trident is the protector, representing fire and three flames. It stands for purity, light and knowledge.

Singing, drumming and dancing are used to acclaim the Mother and anklets are jingled in praise of her holy feet.

The breaking of a coconut represents the cracking of three forms of human weakness – egotism (the hard shell), delusion (the fibre) and material attachments (the outermost covering). The white kernel and sweet water represent the pure soul within.

OTHER LANGUAGES

However, you can susbstitute English 't' and 'd' for the retroflex equivalents and still be understood.

There are also two 'r' sounds that differ from English 'r'. In the first, written as r, the tongue touches the ridge above the upper teeth and is flapped quickly forward, similar to the way English speakers say the 't' sound in 'butter' when speaking quickly. In the second, written as ṛ, the tongue is curled back touching the roof of the mouth (as with the retroflex sounds) and then flapped forward. You can sometimes substitute English 'rd' for this sound. Finally, there are aspirated consonants, which end with a puff of breath. In Fijian Hindi, aspiration is important in distinguishing meaning and is shown with an h following the consonant.

pul	bridge	phul	flower
kālā	black	khālā	valley
tāli	clapping	thāli	brass plate

Other aspirated consonants are:

bh	as in 'grab him' said quickly
ch	as in 'church hat' said quickly
ḍh	as in 'mad house'
gh	as in 'slug him'
jh	as in 'bridge house'
ṭh	as in 'out house'

Note that some books use a different system of transcription. For example, aa might be used for ā and T, D, R for ṭ, ḍ and ṛ.

FIJIAN INDIAN LITERATURE

Fiji Indians write poetry in both Hindi and in English. Some important writers include Subramani, Satendra Nandan, Raymond Pillai and Prem Banfal. The theme of the injustice of the indenture experience rates highly in Fiji-Indian literature, showing its importance on the psyche.

Meeting People

There are no exact equivalents to 'hello' and 'goodbye' in Fijian Hindi. The most common greeting is Kaise 'How are you?'. The usual reply is ṭik 'fine'. A common farewell is fir milegā, meaning 'we'll meet again'.

In more formal contexts, namaste can be used for Hindus, and salām alaikum for Muslims (the reply is alaikum salām).

There aren't any exact equivalents for 'please' and 'thank you' in Fijian Hindi. The polite way of making requests is to use the word thoṛā 'a little', together with a special form of the verb ending in -nā.

Please pass the salt.	thoṛā	nimak	denā
	a little	salt	give

For thank you, people often just say achā 'good'. The word dhanyavād is used to give special thanks to someone who has done something special for you. It means something like 'blessings be bestowed upon you', so you wouldn't want to use it when someone just passes the salt!

FALSE FRIENDS

book	friend
book/ magazine/ pamphlet	sexual partner
gate	motor
field/paddock	car

Visiting a Family

In rural areas, men and women generally eat and socialise separately. Many Indian men enjoy drinking yaqona (kava) as much as other Fijians. However, it isn't customary for guests to bring yaqona with them. If you want to bring something, some sweets for the children are usually appreciated. Some men also drink alcohol after their yaqona,

---

FIRE WALKING

Hindu fire walking is a religious sacrament performed mostly by descendants of southern Indians. Participants aim to become one with the Mother. Their bodies should be enslaved to the spirit and denied all comforts. They believe life is like walking on fire – a disciplined approach, like the one required in the ceremony, helps achieve a balanced life, self-acceptance and an ability to see good in everything.

The fire-walking ceremony is the climax of an annual religious festival, celebrated at many temples throughout Fiji, and held on a full moon in July or August and lasting 10 days.

In the days leading up to the ceremony, the fire walkers forgo sex and meat, and meditate to worship the goddess Maha Devi. They dress in red and yellow to symbolise the cleansing of physical and spiritual impurity, and smear their faces with yellow tumeric to symbolise prosperity and power over disease.

On the day of the ceremony, participants at the Mariamma Temple in Suva have their cheeks, tongues and bodies pierced with three-pronged skewers and are whipped both before and during the ceremony. If they are focused on the divine Mother, they should not feel pain. Participants walk along the pit, which is filled with charred wood rakes over glowing coals, about five times, accompanied by sacred chanting and drumming.

OTHER LANGUAGES

which is called 'washdown'. Female visitors who want to join in may be considered honorary men for the occasion. The custom throughout Fiji is to finish drinking yaqona and/or alcohol before the meal, which can mean some very late dinners!

Festivals

Hindu Holi or Festival of Colours
 held in February or March, when people squirt coloured
 water at each other

Ram Naumi
 Hindu religious festival and party to celebrate the birth of
 Lord Rama, held on the shores of Suva Bay in March or April

Diwali Festival or Festival of Lights
 in October or November, many Hindus worship Lakshmi,
 the goddess of wealth and prosperity, decorating their houses
 and settling outstanding business

Numbers

1	ek
2	dui
3	tin
4	čār
5	pānch
6	chhe
7	sāt
8	āṭh
9	nau
10	das
11	gyārā
12	bāra
100	sau
1000	hazār

English is generally used for numbers between 20 and 99.

PACIFIC FRENCH

French is the official language of New Caledonia, and is one of the offical languages of French Polynesia, including Tahiti. Although much of the Tahitian tourist industry uses English, in more remote and less tourist-oriented islands where Tahitian dialects are spoken, it's definitely useful to know some French.

All French nouns are either masculine or feminine, and adjectives change their form to agree with the noun. In the following list of words and phrases, just the masculine singular version of nouns and adjectives are given.

Pronunciation

For English speakers, there are a few peculiarities in the pronunciation of French .

ai	like the 'e' in 'pet'. Any single consonant following this sound is usually silent.
eau/au	like the 'au' in 'caught' but shorter
ll	pronounced as 'y' – billet is pronounced *bee-yeh*
ch	always pronounced as 'sh'
qu	pronounced 'k'
r	rolled at the back of the throat

There's a distinction between u (as in tu) and ou (as in tout). For both sounds, the lips are rounded and pushed forward, but for the u sound try to say the sound *ee* while keeping the lips pursed. The ou sound is pronounced like the 'oo' in 'cook'.

For nasal vowels the breath escapes partly through the nose. They occur where a syllable ends in a single 'n' or 'm' – the 'n' or 'm' is silent but indicates the nasalisation of the preceding vowel.

You Should Know

Yes.	Oui.
No.	Non.
Maybe.	Peut-être.
Please.	S'il vous plaît.
Thank you (very much).	Merci (beaucoup).

OTHER LANGUAGES

You're welcome.	Je vous en prie.
Excuse me.	Excusez-moi.
I'm sorry (Forgive me).	Pardon.
Hello/Good morning.	Bonjour.
Good evening.	Bonsoir.
Goodbye.	Au revoir.

Meeting People

How are you?	Comment allez-vous?
I'm fine, thanks.	Je vais bien, merci.
What's your name?	Comment vous appelez-vous?
My name's ...	Je m'appelle ...
I understand.	Je comprends.
I don't understand.	Je ne comprends pas.
Could you please write that down?	Est-ce que vous pouvez l'écrire?

Getting Around

I want to go to ...	Je voudrais aller à ...
What time does the ... leave/arrive?	À quelle heure part/ arrive le ...?
boat/ferry	le bateau/le bac
bus	le bus
aeroplane	l'avion
Where's the ...?	Où est ...?
bus station	la gare routiê're
bus stop	l'arrêt d'autobus
ticket office	le guichet
I'd like a ...	Je voudrais ...
one-way ticket	un billet aller simple
return ticket	un billet aller et retour
timetable	un horaire

I'd like to hire a ...	Je voudrais louer ...
bicycle	un vélo
car	une voiture
guide	un guide

Directions

How do I get to ... ?	Comment peut-on aller à ...?
Is it near/far?	Est-ce près/loin d'ici?
(Go) straight ahead.	(Allez) tout droit.
(Turn) left/right ...	(Tournez à) gauche/droite ...
at the traffic lights	aux feux
at the next corner	au coin suivant
What ... is this?	C'est quel (m)/quelle (f) ... ?
street/road	rue/route (f)
suburb	faubourg (m)
town	ville (f)

north	nord
south	sud
east	est
west	ouest

Accommodation

I'm looking for a ...	Je cherche ...
youth hostel	une auberge de jeunesse
camping ground	un camping
hotel	un hôtel
I'd like to book a ...	Je voudrais réserver ...
bed	un lit
single room	une chambre simple
double room	une chambre double
room with a bathroom	une chambre avec salle de bain
I'd like to share a dorm.	Je voudrais partager un dortoir.

OTHER LANGUAGES

How much is it ...?	C'est combien ...?
per night	par nuit
per person	par personne

Around Town

Where's ...?	Où est ...?
I'm looking for a/the ...	Je cherche ...
bank	une banque
... embassy	l'ambassade de ...
hospital	l'hôpital
police	la police
post office	le bureau de poste
telephone box	une cabine téléphonique
tourism office	l'office de tourisme
town hall	la mairie; l'hôtel de ville
What time does it open/close?	Quelle est l'heure d'ouverture; de fermeture?

SIGNS

Gare Routière	Bus Station
Fermé	Closed
Entrée	Entrance
Sortie	Exit
Gare Maritime	Ferry Terminal
Renseignements	Information
Ouvert	Open
La Police	Police
Le Commissariat	Police Station
Interdit	Prohibited
Chambres Libres	Rooms Available
Toilettes/WC	Toilets

OTHER LANGUAGES

I'd like to make a telephone call.	Je voudrais téléphoner.
I'd like to change some (money/travellers cheques).	Je voudrais changer de (la monnaie/des chèques de voyage).

Food

breakfast	le petit déjeuner
lunch	le déjeuner
dinner	le dîner
set dish of the day	le plat du jour
three-course meal offered at set price	menu (du jour)
bakery	la boulangerie
butcher's	la boucherie
café-style snack bar	la brasserie
food shop	l'alimentation
grocery store	l'épicerie
restaurant	le restaurant
shop	le magasin
supermarket	le supermarché
I'm a vegetarian.	Je suis végétarien (m) végétarienne (f).

Shopping

How much is it?	C'est combien?
Can I look at it?	Puis-je le voir?
It's too expensive for me.	C'est trop cher pour moi.
bookshop	la librairie
chemist (pharmacy)	la pharmacie
clothing store	le magasin de vêtements
community clinic	dispensaire
laundry	la laverie

| market | le marché |
| newsagency | l'agence de presse |

Diving

You'll find that most dive centres are used to dealing with English speakers, but the following French terms may be useful.

a dive	une plongée
dive centre	un centre de plongée
diving licence	un brevet de plongée
drift dive	une plongée à la dérive
air tanks	des bouteilles de plongée
flippers	des palmes
mask	un masque
regulator	un détendeur
snorkel	un tuba
wetsuit	une combinaison de plongée
weight belt	une ceinture de plomb

Time & Dates

At what time?	À quelle heure?
What time is it?	Quelle heure est-il?
What's the date?	Quel jour sommes-nous?
When?	Quand?

today	aujourd'hui
tonight	ce soir
tomorrow	demain
yesterday	hier

Monday	lundi
Tuesday	mardi
Wednesday	mercredi
Thursday	jeudi
Friday	vendredi
Saturday	samedi
Sunday	dimanche

OTHER LANGUAGES

Numbers

1	un
2	deux
3	trois
4	quatre
5	cinq
6	six
7	sept
8	huit
9	neuf
10	dix
20	vingt
30	trente
40	quarante
50	cinquante
60	soixante
70	soixante-dix
80	quatre-vingts
90	quatre-vingt-dix
100	cent
1000	mille
2000	deux mille

Health

I need a doctor.	J'ai besoin d'un médecin.
Where's a hospital?	Où est l'hôpital?

I'm ...	Je suis ...
asthmatic.	asthmatique
diabetic	diabétique
pregnant	enceinte

I have (a/an) ...	J'ai ...
asthma	l'asthme
diarrhoea	la diarrhée
earache	mal aux oreilles
headache	mal à la tête

infection	une infection
rash	une rougeur; de l'urticaire
stomachache	mal au ventre

I'm allergic to ...	Je suis allergique aux ...
antibiotics	antibiotiques
penicillin	à la pénicilline
antiseptic	l'antiseptique
aspirin	l'aspirine
condoms	des préservatifs
medicine	le médicament
sanitary napkins	des serviettes hygiéniques
sunscreen	de la crème haute protection
tampons	des tampons

Emergencies

Help!	Au secours!
Call a doctor/ambulance!	Appelez un médecin/une ambulance!
Call the police!	Appelez la police!
Go away!	Vas t'en!
I've been robbed.	On m'a volé (m)/volée (f)
I've been raped.	J'ai été violée.
I'm lost.	Je me suis égaré (m)/égarée (f)

I've lost ...	J'ai perdu ...
... was/were stolen.	On m'a volé ...
my bags	mes bagages
my handbag	mon sac à main
my money	mon argent
my passport	mon passeport
my travellers cheques	mes chèques de voyage

OTHER LANGUAGES

SPANISH

Spanish is Easter Island's official language, and although some tour guides and hotel staff speak English, a basic knowledge of Spanish will be helpful at the airport, bank, hospital or when shopping.

Pronunciation

In Spanish, letters are generally pronounced as they're written. Pronunciation of the letters f, k, l, n, p, q, s and t is virtually identical with English, and y is identical when used as a consonant. The combination ll makes up a separate letter, pronounced as a 'y' and coming after 'l' in the alphabet. Ch and ñ are also separate letters – in the alphabet they come after 'c' and 'n' respectively.

Vowels

Spanish vowels are consistent, and have equivalents in English.

a   as the 'a' in 'father'
e   as the 'e' in 'met';
    at the end of a word it's like the 'ey' in 'hey'
i   as the 'ee' in 'feet'
o   as the 'o' in 'for'
u   as the 'oo' in 'boot';
    after consonants other than 'q', it's more like English 'w'
y   is a consonant except when it stands alone or appears at the
    end of a word, in which case its pronunciation is identical to
    Spanish 'i'

Consonants

Spanish consonants generally resemble their English equivalents, but there are some major exceptions.

b   like the 'b' in 'boot'. Isn't distinguished from 'v'. The letter
    b is referred to in Spanish as 'b larga'.
c   as the 's' in 'see' when it appears before 'e' and i;
    as the 'k' in 'kite' before 'a', 'e' and 'u'
d   closely resembles 'th' in 'feather'

g	like a guttural English 'h' when it appears before 'e' and 'i'; as the 'g' in 'go' when it appears before 'a', 'o' and 'u'
h	is invariably silent; if your name begins with this letter, listen carefully when immigration officials summon you to pick up your passport
j	most closely resembles English 'h', but is slightly more guttural
ñ	like 'ni' in 'onion'
r	nearly identical to English 'r' except at the beginning of a word, when it's often rolled
rr	very strongly rolled
v	resembles English 'v', but see 'b', above. Referred to in Spanish as 'b corta'.
x	as the 'x' in 'taxi', except in a few words for which it's pronounced as 'j'
z	as the 's' in 'sun'

Stress

Stress, often indicated by visible accents (such as á), is very important, since it can change the meaning of a word. In general, words ending in vowels or the letters n or s have stress on the second-last syllable, while those with other endings have stress on the last syllable. Thus vaca (cow) and caballos (horses) both have stress on their second-last syllables.

Visible accents, which can occur anywhere in a word, dictate stress over these general rules. Thus sótano (basement), América and porción (portion) all have the stress on the syllable with the accented vowel. When words are written all in capitals, the accent is often not shown, but it still affects the pronunciation.

Meeting People

Hello.	Hola.
Good morning.	Buenos días.
Good afternoon.	Buenas tardes.
Good evening; good night.	Buenas noches.
Goodbye.	Adiós.

Please.	Por favor.
Thank you.	Gracias.
You're welcome.	De nada.

Useful Words & Phrases

Yes.	Sí.
No.	No.
and	y
to/at	a
for	por/para
of/from	de/desde
in	en
with	con
without	sin
Where?	Dónde?
Where is ...?	Dónde está ...?
Where are ...?	Dónde están ...?
How much?	Cuanto?
How many?	Cuantos?
How?	Cómo?
When?	Cuando?

before	antes
after	después
soon	pronto
already	ya
now	ahora
right away	en seguida; al tiro
here	aquí
there	allí

I understand.	Entiendo.
I don't understand.	No entiendo.
I don't speak much Spanish.	No hablo mucho castellano.

I'd like ...	Me gustaría ...
coffee	café
beer	cerveza
tea	té
water	agua

Getting Around

aeroplane	el avión
bicycle	la bicicleta
bus	el ómnibus/bus
car	el auto
horse	el caballo
motorcycle	la motocicleta
truck	camión

toilet	baño/servicios
men's	hombres/caballeros/varones
women's	señoras/damas

Accommodation

Is there ...?; Are there ...?	Hay ...?
What does it cost?	Cuanto cuesta?
May I see it?	Puedo verlo?
I don't like it.	No me gusta.

It's fine, I'll take it.	Vale, la alquilo.
the bill	la cuenta
double/single room	habitación doble/single
too expensive	demasiado caro
hotel	hotel/residencial
per night	por noche

Post & Telephone

airmail	correo aéreo
collect call	cobro revertido
letter	carta
parcel	paquete
post office	correo
registered mail	certificado
stamps	estampillas

Geographical Terms

bay	bahía
bridge	puente
farm	fundo
hill	cerro
lake	lago
marsh	estero
mountain	cerro
pass	paso
river	río
waterfall	cascada/salto

Health

Rapa Nui has a hospital staffed with medical personnel from Chile, so once at the hospital any emergencies will be dealt with in Spanish. There's no pharmacy on the island, so medication (even aspirin) must be obtained at the hospital.

I'm ill.	Estoy enferma/o.
I need a doctor.	Necesito una doctora/ un doctor.

OTHER LANGUAGES

Where's the nearest ...?	¿Dónde está ... más cercano?
doctor	el médico
hospital	el hospital
chemist	la famacia
dentist	el dentista

I feel ...	Me siento ...
dizzy	mareada/o
shivery	destemplada/o
weak	débil

I feel nauseous.   Tengo náuseas.

I have (a/an)...	Tengo ...
allergy	alergia
bronchitis	bronquitis
burn	una quemadura
cold	un resfriado; catarro
constipation	estreñimiento
diarrhoea	diarrea
fever	fiebre
headache	dolor de cabeza
indigestion	indigestión
infection	una infección
inflammation	una inflamación
pain	dolor
rash	irritación
STD	una enfermedad de transmisión sexual
stomachache	dolor de estómago
sunburn	una quemadura de sol
travel sickness	mareo

Time & Dates

Eight o'clock is las ocho, while 8.30 is las ocho y treinta (lit: eight and thirty) or las ocho y media (eight and a half). However, 7.45 is las ocho menos quince (lit: eight minus fifteen) or las ocho menos cuarto (eight minus one quarter).

Times are modified by morning (de la manaña) or afternoon (de la tarde) instead of 'am' or 'pm'. It's also common to use the 24-hour clock, especially with transportation schedules.

Days

Monday	lunes
Tuesday	martes
Wednesday	miércoles
Thursday	jueves
Friday	viernes
Saturday	sábado
Sunday	domingo

Numbers

1	uno
2	dos
3	tres
4	cuatro
5	cinco
6	seis
7	siete
8	ocho
9	nueve
10	diez
11	once
12	doce
13	trece
14	catorce
15	quince
16	dieciseis
17	diecisiete
18	dieciocho

19	diecinueve
20	veinte
21	veintiuno
22	veintidós
23	veintitré
24	veinticuatro
30	treinta
31	treinta y uno
32	treinta y dos
33	treinta y tres
40	cuarenta
41	cuarenta y uno
42	cuarenta y dos
50	cincuenta
60	sesenta
70	setenta
80	ochenta
90	noventa
100	cien
101	ciento uno
102	ciento dos
110	ciento diez
120	ciento veinte
130	ciento treinta
200	doscientos
300	trescientos
400	cuatrocientos
500	quinientos
600	seiscientos
700	setecientos
800	ochocientos
900	novecientos
1000	mil
1100	mil cien
1200	mil doscientos
2000	dos mil

OTHER LANGUAGES

5000	cinco mil
10,000	diez mil
50,000	cincuenta mil
100,000	cien mil
1,000,000	un millón

Emergencies

Help!	¡Socorro!/¡Auxilio!
Call the police!	¡Llame a la policía!
Could you help me please?	¿Puede ayudarme, por favor?
Could I use the telephone please?	¿Puedo usar el teléfono, por favor?
Fire!	¡Fuego!
Look out!	¡Ojo!
Call a doctor!	¡Llame a un médico!
Go away!	¡Váyase!
I'll call the police!	¡Voy a llamar a la policía!
I've been robbed!	¡Me han robado!
I'm lost.	Estoy perdido/a.
I've lost ...	He perdido ...
My ... was stolen.	Me robaron mi(s) ...
bags	maletas
handbag	bolso
money	dinero
passport	pasaporte
travellers cheques	cheques de viaje

PACIFIC ENGLISHES

New Zealand English

As everywhere in the world where English is spoken, in New Zealand it is spoken in a unique way. The elision of vowels is the most distinctive feature of the Kiwi pronunciation of English. The New Zealand treatment of 'fish 'n' chips', for example, is an endless source of delight for Australians when pronounced *fush 'n chups*. In the North Island, sentences often have eh attached to the end. In the far south, a rolled r is widely practised. A holdover from that region's Scottish heritage, it is especially noticeable in Southland.

afghan
  a popular home-made chocolate biscuit

All Black
  a revered member of the national rugby team. The name comes from 'All Blacks', which the New Zealand rugby team were called by the press on an early visit to England

bach
  holiday home, usually a wooden cottage (pronounced *batch*)

the barrier
  local name for Great Barrier Island in the Hauraki Gulf

Beehive
  Parliament House in Wellington, so called because of its distinctive shape

black-water rafting
  rafting or tubing underground in a cave or tomo (cave entrance)

box of birds
  usually a reply to 'How are you', meaning 'on top of the world'

bro
  (lit: brother) usually meaning 'mate', as in 'just off to see the bros'

OTHER LANGUAGES

bush
heavily forested areas

Captain Cooker
large feral pig, introduced by Captain Cook and now roaming wild over most of New Zealand's rugged bush land

choice
fantastic/great

ciggies
cigarettes

crib
the name for a bach (holiday home) in Otago and Southland

cuzzies
cousins; relatives in general

chillie bin
cooler/esky (large insulated box for keeping beer and other drinks cold)

dairy
a small corner store which sells just about everything, especially milk, bread, the newspaper and ice cream; a convenience store

domain
open-grassed area in a town or city. Often the site of gardens, picnic areas and bowling clubs.

doss house
temporary accommodation

farmstay
accommodation on a typical Kiwi farm where you're encouraged to join in the day-to-day activities

fiscal envelope
money set aside by the New Zealand government to make financial reparation for injustices to Maori people since the Treaty of Waitangi

football
  rugby, either union or league

freezing works
  slaughterhouse/abattoir

Godzone
  New Zealand (God's own)

good as (gold)
  very good

greenstone
  jade/pounamu

handle
  a beer glass with a handle

hard case
  an unusual or strong character

hokey pokey
  neither mischief nor magic but a delicious variety of ice cream

homestay
  accommodation in a family house where you're treated, for better or for worse, as one of the family

hooray
  a rather 'bush' way of saying goodbye

huntaway
  loud-barking sheepherding dog, usually a sturdy black-and-brown hound

Instant Kiwi
  state-run lottery

Interislander
  the ferry which makes the crossing between the North and South islands across Cook Strait

Is it what!
  strong affirmation or agreement; Yes isn't it!

OTHER LANGUAGES

jandals
  sandals/flip flops/thongs

jersey
  jumper/sweater; the shirt worn by rugby players

judder bars
  speed humps (bumps in the road designed to make you
  drive slowly)

kiwi
  a flightless brown bird with a long beak. The Kiwi is the
  national symbol and the name by which New Zealanders
  often refer to themselves. It's also an adjective which means
  anything of or relating to New Zealand. Also a member of
  the national Rugby League team.

kiwi fruit
  a small, succulent fruit with fuzzy brown skin and juicy
  green flesh (once called 'Chinese gooseberries')

lounge bar
  more upmarket bar than a public bar

metal/metalled road
  gravel road

motor camp
  holiday place with sites for tents, caravans and campervans as
  well as on-site caravans, cabins and tourist flats

Nifty-fifty
  50 cc motorcycle

Pacific Rim
  term used to describe modern New Zealand cuisine; cuisine
  with an innovative use of local produce, especially seafood,
  with imported styles

Pakeha
  a fair-skinned person of European ancestry

parapenting
paragliding

pillocking
'surfing' across mud flats on a rubbish bin lid

Plunket
the Plunket Society is an organisation established to promote the health of babies. There are Plunket rooms (baby clinics), Plunket nurses (baby nurses) and so on.

polly
politician

ponga
(pronounced *pahngah*) silver tree fern. The ponga is called a bungy (pronounced *bungee* with a soft 'g') in parts of the South Island.

pushchair
baby stroller

quad bikes
four-wheeled farm bikes

rap jump
face-down abseil

raupo
bullrush (a grass found in marshes)

Rheiny
affectionate term for Rheineck beer

rigger
half-gallon plastic bottle used for holding draught beer

section
small block of land

silver fern
    the symbol worn on the jerseys of the All Blacks, representing
    the underside of a ponga leaf

Steinie
    affectionate term for Steinlager beer

tarseal
    the bitumen surface of a road

tramp
    walk/trek/hike

varsity
    university

wopwops
    to be in the wopwops is to be in the middle of nowhere

Norfolk

Norfolk Island lies in the middle of the Pacific Ocean. It's the
largest of a cluster of three islands emerging from the Norfolk
Ridge, which stretches from New Zealand to New Caledonia.

English is Norfolk Island's official language and is the first
language of Norfolk Islanders, although Norfolk is still spoken
among Pitcairn descendants. Although you won't be expected to
speak Norfolk while on the island, the following words and phrases
should give you some idea of what the language sounds like. All
sounds in Norfolk are similar to those found in English, except
for 'g', which is always pronounced as the 'g' in 'get'.

THEY MAY SAY ...

Galp yu self to some
wettles, doo waet
– bog een!

Help yourself to some
food, don't wait
– start eating!

Little is known about the island's history before it was sighted by Captain Cook in 1774. After two stints as a British penal colony in the 18th and 19th centuries, in 1865 it was handed over to the 194 descendants of the mutineers from the *HMS Bounty*, who had outgrown their native Pitcairn Island. Although some returned to Pitcairn, the majority remained, and make up about a third of the current population of 2000 Norfolk Islanders.

Greetings

How are you?	Whutta waye?
Hi, how are you?	Hey brud, whuttawaye? (brud is similar to 'mate' in Australia)
How are you all?	All yorlye gwen?

Food

anna	local dish made from cold sweet potatoes (kumeras) and coconut milk
bescet	biscuit
cherry moyah	custard apple
gudda	boiled green bananas
gwarwa	yellow guava
hihi pie	periwinkle pie
melk	milk
moree	steamed pudding made with pastry and fresh fruit, such as mulberries or red guava
mudda	banana dumplings, made from grated green bananas

PRONOUNS	
myse	my
yu	you
yoos	your
hi	he (the 'i' sounds like the 'i' in 'hit')
hem	he/him
dem	they/them/their

OTHER LANGUAGES

KINGSTON

Kingston, Norfolk's town, is referred to simply as Toun by Norfolk Islanders.

mullun	melon
pilhai	baked kumera (sweet potatoes)
plun	banana(s)
porpaye	red guava
potagee	species of sweet potato thought to have been brought to the island by Portuguese sailors who visited Norfolk Island on American whaling ships
soop	soup; home brew made from malt and yeast
tarla	taro (edible tuber)
tayte	sweet potato

The Sea

suff	sea/surf/waves
suff comen een	rising tide
suff sinken	falling tide
suff se dunna sink	low tide
suff se gude	calm sea

OTHER LANGUAGES

DID YOU KNOW ... The term saelo originally meant 'sail sighted'. In whaling days, as soon as a boat harpooned a whale, a flag was hoisted to warn other boats and islanders watching from the clifftop that help might be needed. Today, saelo is used to draw attention to something ridiculous.

ENCOUNTER WITH LOGAN

Logan was a Norfolk Island horse that kicked anything within kicking distance, causing an emormous amount of breakages and injuries. The Norfolk expression Logan se kick et means that someone or something looks terrible, as though they've encountered Logan.

Festivals

Agricultural & Horticultural Annual Show

held every October since 1860, this event showcases Norfolk Islander arts and crafts, photography, food, agricultural products and animals

Bounty Day

re-enactment of the landing of the Islanders' Pitcairn ancestors at Kingston Jetty on 8 June 1856, followed by a picnic at Slaughter Bay within the grounds of the former prison. Celebrations kick on with the Bounty Ball.

Foundation Day

holiday on 6 March marks the first European (convict) settlement of Norfolk Island in 1788, with a re-enactment of the landing

Hibiscus Festival

Thanksgiving Day has been celebrated in the style of a harvest festival since American whalers began visiting the island in the 19th century

Pitkern

Pitkern is a dialect of English that began developing when nine mutineers from the *HMS Bounty* together with 19 Tahitian men, women and children settled on uninhabited Pitcairn Island in 1790. Although uninhabited when the mutineers arrived, it is believed there was a Polynesian settlement on the island between the 12th and 15th centuries, such as a quarry for the stones used to make adzes and other cutting tools, marae platforms and images when the mutineers arrived. Pitcairn Islanders speak English as their first language and English is used in education.

Due to overcrowding, in 1856 the entire population of 194 moved to Norfolk Island, but two years later, 16 returned to Pitcairn and were followed by four more families in 1864, bringing the population up to 43. The current population is around 50, although there are many more Pitcairners residing overseas.

Meeting People

How are you?	What a way you?
I'm glad to meet you.	I glad to meet yorley.
Where are you going?	By you given?;
	About you gwen?
Good!	Cooshoo!
Never mind.	Do mine.
(common insult)	You'sa dirty dawg.
(humerous threat)	You'sa daid as a hatchet growin' fahs!
Looks like it's going to rain.	Semme thing given rain.
What do you want?	What thing you want?
Never mind.	Do mine.
Let it be.	Lub be.
I don't think so.	I nor believe.
No smoking here.	Cah smoke yah.
How often do ships call here?	Humuch shep corl ya?
That ship's not going to stop at Pitcairn.	Da shep es ay los' bawl.

Food

Would you like to come to dinner?	You like-a come down ours fer suppa?
I'm going to cook up some food.	I gwen whihi up some wettles.

What food grows   Wut weckle groos
   on Pitcarin?   ana Pitkern?

When something's unpalatable ...

Want a break for eat it. (lit: only a bird would eat it)
Want a tongs for eat it.

coconut	cocknut
banana	plum/plun
dumplings	mudda
potato	tayte
red guavas	porpay
sweet potato	kumara

Placenames

Adams's Rock
   large rock just east of Bounty Bay named in honour of John
   Adams, the Island patriarch

Bang on Iron
   location on the north-east coastal road west of Adamstown,
   where mutineers set up a forge under an overhanging rock

Bounty Bay
   shallow indentation in the north-eastern coastline east of
   Adamstown, where HMS *Bounty* landed and was later
   burned

Christian's Cave
   cave frequented by Fletcher Christian went when he wanted
   privacy, located at the northern end of Palva Walley

Down the God
   point on the coast between Where Freddie Fall and Pool of
   Uaro, where heathen idols were found and cast into the sea

Down the Rope
   steep cliff on the southern coast with Pitcairn's only beach at its
   foot. In the early days, a rope was strung down the cliff face to
   help Islanders descend more easily. Also known as The Rope

OTHER LANGUAGES

Hill of Difficulty
  steep trail up to Adamstown, which is perched 120 metres above the sea

John Catch a Cow
  relatively flat area of land in the southern part of the island

Johnny Fall
  place on the northen coast where John Mills fell to his death

No Guts Captain
  the burial spot of the captain of a visiting ship who asked not to be buried at sea. Pitcairn was the next landfall, and he was buried there.

Pitcairn Island
  named after Midshipman Robert Pitcairn, who first spotted the island

Six Feet
  dangerous reef in the area of Young's Rocks

Tedside
  the western coast of Pitcairn. The name developed from 'the other side'.

Where Dan Fall
  spot on the northern coast where Daniel McCoy, grandson of mutineer William McCoy, fell to his death in 1855

Where Minnie Off
  the place where Minnie Christian was washed from the rocks by a big wave, and then rescued

OTHER LANGUAGES

FURTHER READING

FIJIAN

Reed, A. & I. Hames (1967) *Myths & Legends of Fiji & Rotuma*, Reed

Milner, G. (1956) *Fijian Grammar*, Government Press, Suva

Schutz, A. (1979) *Spoken Fijian*, University Press of Hawaii, Honolulu

HAWAIIAN

Elbert, S. & M. Kawena Pukui (1986) *Hawaiian Dictionary*, University of Hawaii Press

Elbert, S. & M. Kawena Pukui (1979) *Hawaiian Grammar*, University of Hawaii Press

Helbig, R. (1970) *Let's Learn a Little Hawaiian*, Hawaiian Service

Hopkins, A. (1992) *Ka Lei Ha'aheo*, University of Hawaii Press

Kahananui, D. & A. Anthony (1978) *E Kama'ilio Hawai'i Kakou*, University of Hawai'i Press

Pukui, M. (1983) *'... lelo No'eau: Hawaiian Proverbs and Poetical Sayings*. Bishop Museum Special Publication Number 71.

Pukui, M., E. Haertig & C. Lee (1972) *Nānā I Ke Kumu: Look to the Source*, Vols 1 & 2, Hui Hānai

Schutz, A. (1994) *The Voices of Eden: A History of Hawaiian Studies*, University of Hawai'i Press

Snakenburg, R. (1988) *The Hawaiian Sentence Book*, The Bess Press

MAORI

Armstrong, A. (1986) *Say It in Maori*, Seven Seas Publishing

Biggs, B. (1992) *The Complete English-Maori Dictionary*, Auckland University Press

Biggs, B. (1992) *English-Maori – Maori-English Dictionary*, Auckland University Press

Ihimaera, W. (ed.) (1993) Te Ao Marama , Contemporary Maori Writing, Vol 2: *He Whakaatanga o te Ao – The Reality*, Reed

Ihimaera, W. (ed.) (1992) Te Ao Marama, Contemporary Maori Writing, Vol 1: *Te Whakahuatanga o te Ao – Reflections of Reality*, Reed

Reed, A. (1992) *A Dictionary of Maori Place Names* (2nd edn), Reed Books

Ryan, P. (1993) *The Revised Dictionary of Modern Maori* (3rd edn), Heinemann Education

Tauroa, P. (1990) *Collins Maori Phrase Book*, Collins

Williams, H. (1957) The *Dictionary of the Maori Language* (6th edn), RE Owen, Government Printer, Wellington

RAPANUI

Du Feu, V. (1996) *Grammar of Rapanui*, Routledge

Du Feu, V. (1993) Modern Rapanui Language: Retention and Survival, in S. Fischer (ed.) *Easter Island Studies*, Oxbow Books, pp. 172–3

Du Feu, V. and S. Fischer (1993) The Rapanui Language, in S. Fischer (ed.) *Easter Island Studies*, Oxbow Press, pp. 165–8

Englert, S. (1978) *Idioma Rapanui: Gramatica y diccionario del antigua idioma de la Isla de Pascua* (2nd edn), Ediciones de la Universidad de Chile

Englert, S. (1970) *Island at the Center of the World*, Scribner's

Englert, S. (1938) *Diccionario rapanui-español*, Universidad de Chile

Fischer, S. (1997) *Rongorongo: The Easter Island Script, History, Tradition, Texts*, Oxford University Press

Fuentes, J. (1960) *Dictionary & Grammar of the Easter Island Language*, Editorial Andres Bello (Spanish/English)

Haoa R., A. Betty & W. Liller (1996) *Speak Rapanui! ¡Hable Rapanui!. The Language of Easter Island*, Easter Island Foundation

Langdon, R. & D. Tryon (1983) *The Language of Easter Island: Its Development and eastern Polynesian Relationships.* Institute for Polynesian Studies, Brigham Young University, Hawaii

Métraux, A. (1940) *Ethnology of Easter Island*, Bulletin 160 of the Bernice P. Bishop Museum, Honolulu

RAROTONGAN MAORI

Buse, J. with Raututi Taringa (1995) *Cook Islands Maori Dictionary*, Ministry of Education, Rarotonga

Crocombe, M., R. Crocombe, K. Kauraka & M. Tongia (eds) (1992) *Te Rau Maire: Poems and Stories of the Pacific*, Cook Islands Ministry of Cultural Development, Rarotonga and University of the South Pacific, Suva

Herrmann, J. (1988) *E Au Imene Tamataora: Songs and Song writers of the Cook Islands*, University of the South Pacific, Suva

Jonassen, J. (1992) *The Ghost at Tokatarava and Other Stories from the Cook Islands*, Ministry of Cultural Development, Rarotonga

Jonassen, J. (1981) *Cook Islands Legends*, University of the South Pacific, Suva

Kauraka K. (1991) *Tales of Manihiki*, University of the South Pacific, Suva

Kauraka K. (1989) *Oral Tradition in Manihiki*, University of the South Pacific, Suva

Kauraka Kauraka (1983) *Legends from the Atolls*, University of the South Pacific, Suva

MacCauley, J. *Te Ata O Ikurangi – The Shadow of IkurangiI*, Cook Islands Library & Museum Society, Rarotonga

Rere, T. (1980) *Conversational Maori*, Rarotonga

FURTHER READING

Savage, S. (1980) *A Dictionary of the Maori Language of Rarotonga*, University of the South Pacific, Suva

Strickland, M. (1979) *Say it in Rarotongan*, Pacific Publications

Tepuaotera Turepu Carpentier, T. & C. Beaumonth (1995), *Kai Korero: A Cook Islands Maori Language Coursebook*, Pasifika Press, Auckland

Tongia, M. (1977, reprinted1991) *Korero*, Mana Publications

SAMOAN

Allardice, R. (1985) *A simplified dictionary of modern Samoan*, Polynesian Press, Auckland

Downs, E. (1942) *Everyday Samoan*, The North Shore Gazette Ltd

Duranti, A. (1994) *From grammar to politics: Linguistic anthropology in a Western Samoa village*, University of California Press

Figiel, S. (1998) *Where We Once Belonged*, Viking

Figiel, S. (1996) *The Girl in the Moon Circle*, Mana Publications, Suva

Hunkin, G. (1988) *Gagana Samoa: A Samoan language coursebook*, Polynesian Press

Johnson, A. & L. Harmon (1972) *Let's speak Samoan*, Church of Jesus Christ of the Latter-Day Saints Press

Kasiano, AS. (1991) *Gagana Samoa mo Pisikoa: Peace Corps Samoan language handbook*, Peace Corps Training Staff

Mailo, S. (1972) *Pale Fuiono*, parts I & II, Pagopago, American Samoa

Marsack, C. (1962) *Teach yourself Samoan*, The English Universities Press Limited

Mayer, J. (1976) *Samoan Language*, United States Peace Corps

Milner, G. (1966) *Samoan dictionary*, Oxford University Press

Milner, G. (1961) The Samoan vocabulary of respect. *Journal of the Anthropological Institute of Great Britain and Ireland* (91), pp. 296–317

Mosel, Ulrike, and Even Hovdhaugen (1992) *Samoan reference grammar*, Scandinavian University Press.

Moyle, R. (1988) *Traditional Samoan music*, Auckland University Press

Moyle, R. (1981) *Fagogo: Fables from Samoa*, Auckland University Press; Oxford University Press

Murdock, G. Jr (1965) *O le va fealoai*, Church of Jesus Christ of Latter-Day Saints

Pratt, Rev. G. (1984) *Grammar and dictionary of the Samoan language* (third edition), Malua Printing Press. (First edition printed 1862, reprinted 1984 by R. McMillan.)

Shore, B. (1982) *Salailua: a Samoan mystery*, Columbia University Press

Shore, B., L. Campbell & U. Petaia (1973) *Conversational Samoan* (Books I & II) United States Peace Corps

Steubel, C., Brother Herman & I. Toafa (1987) *Tala o le Vavau – The Myths, Legends and Customs of Old Samoa*, Polynesian Press

Tuitele, Moega, and John Kneubuhl. (1978) *Upu Samoa: Samoan words*, Bilingual/Bicultural Education Project of American Samoa

Tuitele, Moega, T. Mila Sapolu, and John Kneubuhl. (1978) *La tatou gagana. Tusi muamua*, Bilingual/Bicultural Education Project of American Samoa

Tu'i, Tatupu Faafetai Mataafa. (1987) *Lauga: Samoan oratory*, University of the South Pacific

Violette, le R. (1879) *Dictionnaire Samoa-Francais-Anglais*, Maissonneuve

FURTHER READING

Wendt, A. (1988) *Flying Fox in a Freedom Tree & Other Stories*, Penguin

Wendt, A. (1987) *Birth and Death of the Miracle Man*, Penguin

Wendt, A. (1987) *Sons for the Return Home*, Penguin

Wendt, A. (1984) *Shaman of Visions*, Auckland University Press; Oxford University Press

Wendt, A. (1981) *Pouliuli,* University Press of Hawaii

Wendt, A. (1979) *Leaves of the Banyan Tree*, Allen Lane

Wendt, A. (1976) *Inside Us the Dead*, Longman Paul

TAHITIAN

Tryon, D. (1970) *Coversational Tahitian: An introduction to the Tahitian language of French Polynesia*, ANU Press. Also available in French as *Parler Tahitien en 24 Leçons* (Editions Octavo).

TONGAN

Churchward, C. (1959) *Tongan Dictionary (English Tongan–Tongan English)*, Oxford University Press

Churchward, C. (1953) *Tongan Grammar*, Vava'u Press

Hau'ofa, E. (1983) *Tales of the Tikongs*, Penguin

Hau'ofa, E. (1987) *Kisses in the Nederends*, Penguin

Helu-Thaman, K. (1981) *Langakali: Poems*, Mana Publications

Helu-Thaman, K. (1980, © 1974) *You, the Choice of My Parents: Poems*, Mana Publications

Shumway, E. (1988) *An Intensive Course in Tongan*, Brigham Young University, Hawaii

OTHER LANGUAGES
Norfolk

Buffett, A. & Laycock, D. (1988) *Speak Norfolk Today*, Languages for Intercultural Communication in the Pacific Area Project of the Australian Academy of the Humanities

Christian, E. (1986) *From Myse Randa: A Selection of Poems and Tales of Norfolk Island*, Norfolk Island

Nobbs Palmer, B. (1992) *A Dictionary of Norfolk Words and Usages plus English-Norfolk appendix*, BN Palmer

Pitkern

Ross, A. & A. Moverly (1964) *The Pitcairnese Language*, Deutsch

MAPS

South Pacific	12-13
Fiji	16
Hawaii	48
New Caledonia	72
New Zealand	94
Niue	118
Easter Island (Rapa Nui)	138
Cook Islands	162
Samoa	178
Tahiti	210
Tonga	232
Pitcairn & Norfolk Islands	254

TEXT

INTRODUCTION	11
Abbreviations	14
FIJIAN	15
Apologies	26
Artefacts	39
Body Language	27
Bus	36
Car	36
Ceremonies, initiation	44
Consonants	20
Country, in the	37
Dates	41
Days	42
Dialects	18
Directions	35
Etiquette	27
Family	28
Festivals	39
Food	32
Local Dishes	33
Forms of Address	25
Geographical Terms	38
Getting Around	35
Greetings	22
Handshakes	21
Health	44, 46
History	17
Introduction	17
Isalei	45
Kava	27-28, 30
Literature	24
Local Dishes	33
Meeting People	22
Months	42
Music, contemporary	37
Names	30
Numbers	42
Polite Speech	22
Pronunciation	19
Requests	26
Seasons	39
Song	45
Souvenirs	39
Time	41
Vowels	19
Yaqona	27-28, 30
HAWAIIAN	47
Animals	60
Artefacts	63
Body Language	52
Cooking, traditional	56
Consonants	50
Dates	69
Days	69
Directions	57
Etiquette	51

Family 52
Festivals 63
Food 55
    Traditional Cooking 56
    Local Foods 56
Geographical Terms 57
Getting Around 57
Gods 53
Greetings 51
Hawai'i Aloha 67
Holidays 63
Hula 65
Introduction 49
Legends 68
Letter Writing 64
Lū'au 55
Meeting People 51
Mongoose 54
Months 69
Myths 68
National Anthem 66
Numbers 70
People 53
Placenames 58
Plants 61
Pronunciation 50
Shaka Sign 69
Song 66, 67
Souvenirs 63
Street Names 59
Surf 62
Time 69
Vowels 50

KANAK LANGUAGES 71
Ajië 87
    Food 87
    Oral History 88
    People 87
    Pronouns 87
Classification 73
Cooking, traditional 79

Consonants 75
Dates 83
Days 83
Etiquette 78
Family 78
Festivals 81-82
Food 79
Getting Around 80
Greetings 76
History 74
Introduction 73
Languages 73
    Ajië 87-90
    Loyalty Islands 74
    Northern 73
    Southern 74
Literature 85
Meeting People 76
Nengone 90
    Numbers 91
    People 90
Numbers 86
People 78
Places 80
Pronouns 83
Pronunciation 75
Time 84-85
Vowels 75
Weather 81

MAORI 93
Artefacts 107
Consonants 97
Dates 112
Days 112
Family 99
Festivals 114
Food 104
Getting Around 104
Greetings 98
Haka 110
History 95

Introduction 95
Legends 108-112
Literature 103
Marae........................ 100-103
Meeting People 98
Months 114
Numbers 114-116
People................................ 98
Placenames 104-107
Pokarekare Ana 113
Pronunciation 96
Seasons 107
Song 113
Souvenirs 107
Time 112
Vowels 96
Warriors 98

NIUEAN 117
Apologies 125
Artefacts 131
Body Language 125
Car 129
Celebrations 131
Consonants 122
Country, in the 130
Dates 133
Days 133
Etiquette 125
Family.............................. 126
Food 128
Forms of Address 124
Geographical Terms 130
Getting Around 129
Greetings 123
History 119
Introduction 119
Literature 129
Meeting People 123
Months 133
Names 135
Numbers 135

Pronunciation 120-123
Seasons 131
Song 134
Souvenirs 131
Time 124, 133
Vowels 120

RAPANUI 137
Ahu 148
Artefacts 146
Birdman 154
Birds 150
Christmas 154
Consonants 141
Dates 157
Days 157
Dia de Independencia 152
Family.............................. 142
Fauna 150
Festivals 152
Flora 150
Food 144
Geographical Terms 147
Getting Around 145
Greetings 142
History 140
Hoto Matu'a 155
Introduction 139
Kavakava 147
Legends 155
Mammals 151
Market, at the 145
Moai 150, 152
Meeting People 142
Months 158
Numbers 158-160
People.............................. 143
Plants 151
Pronouns 158
Pronunciation 140
Questions 149
Rongorongo 155

Sightseeing 146
Souvenirs 146
Tapati Rapanui 152
Time 157
Vowels 141
Weather 149

RAROTONGAN 161
Artefacts 169
Bus 168
Dates 174
Days 174
Family........................ 164
Festivals 171
Food 166
    Local Dishes 167
Geographical Terms 170
Getting Around 168
Gods 165
Greetings 164
Introduction 163
Legends 173
Local Dishes 167
Market, at the 168
Matu Rori 167
Meeting People 164
Months 174
Namesakes 172
Numbers 175
People 165
Pronouns 166
Pronunciation 163
Seasons 170
Souvenirs 169
Time 174
Tumunu 175
Umu 166
Umukai 166
Woodcarving 168

SAMOAN 177
'Ava 187

Animals 197
Artefacts 199
Body Language 184
Ceremony, 'Ava 187
Consonants 181
Currency 207
Dancing 202
Dates 205
Days 205
Dress Codes 189
Etiquette 186
Fa'amatai 190
Fale 195
Family 190
Festivals 201
Fiafia 202
Fono 191
Food 193
    Local Dishes 194
Geographical Terms 196
Getting Around 195
Greetings 185
Holidays 201
Ifoga 183
Introduction 179
Kava 187
Language
    Chiefly 184
    Respect 183
    Taboo 197
Legends 203-205
Literature 202
Local Dishes 194
Market, at the 194
Medicine, traditional 199
Meeting People 183
Months 205
Music 201
Names 198
Nationalities 189
Numbers 206
Pe'a 200

People 188
Plants 198
Pronouns 180
Pronunciation 180
    Colloquial 182
Questions 196
Sa 187
Social Structure 190
Souvenirs 199
Stress 182
Time 206
Vowels 180
Writing 182

TAHITIAN 209
Artefacts 221
Consonants 213
Dance 225
Dates 227
Days 227
Festivals 223
Food 218
    Fish 218
    Sauces 219
    Traditional Dishes 218
Geographical Terms 220
Getting Around 220
Introduction 211
Legends 226
Maeva 224
Marae 226
Market, at the 220
Meeting People 217
Months 227
Music 224
Numbers 228
Pronouns 229
Pronunciation 212
Questions 217
Song 224
Souvenirs 221
Time 228

Vowels 212

TONGAN 231
Artefacts 245
Body Language 239
Consonants 234
Counting 252
Dance 248
Etiquette 240
Fakapale 248
Festivals 246
Food 242
    Local Dishes 242
Forms of Address 237
Geographical Terms 245
Getting Around 244
Greetings 235
Introduction 233
Legends 249
Literature 235
Meeting People 235
Myths 249
National Anthem 247
Numbers 252
People 239
Placenames 244
Pronunciation 233
Relatives 238
Royalty, meeting 236
Souvenirs 245
Time 251
Titles 237
Vowels 233
Writing letters 241

OTHER LANGUAGES 253
Pacific Englishes 279
    New Zealand English 279
    Norfolk 284
    Pitkern 287

Fijian Hindi 255

History 255
Pronunciation 256
Pronouns 256
Symbolic Rites 257
Literature 258
Meeting People 259
Visiting A Family 260
Fire Walking 260
Festivals 261
Numbers 261

Pacific French 262
Accommodation 264
Around Town 265
Dates 267
Directions 264
Diving 267
Emergencies 269
Food 266
Getting Around 263
Health 268
Meeting People 263
Numbers 268
Pronunciation 262
Shopping 266
Signs 265
Time 267

Spanish 270
Accommodation 273
Dates 276
Days 276
Emergencies 278
Geographical Terms 274
Getting Around 273
Health 274
Meeting People 271
Numbers 276
Post 274
Pronunciation 270
Telephone 274
Time 276

FURTHER READING 291
Fijian 293
Hawaiian 293
Maori 293
Norfolk 297
Other Languages 297
Pitkern 297
Rapanui 294
Rarotongan Maori 295
Samoan 296
Tahitian 298
Tongan 298
Other Languages 299

NOTES

NOTES

NOTES

NOTES

NOTES